Bettie Page

THE LOST YEARS

Bettie Page

THE LOST YEARS

AN INTIMATE LOOK AT THE *Queen of Pinups,*

THROUGH HER PRIVATE LETTERS & NEVER-PUBLISHED PHOTOS

TORI RODRIGUEZ

WITH RON BREM

Guilford, Connecticut

An imprint of The Rowman & Littlefield Publishing Group, Inc.
4501 Forbes Blvd., Ste. 200
Lanham, MD 20706
www.rowman.com

Distributed by NATIONAL BOOK NETWORK

British Library Cataloguing in Publication Information available

Library of Congress Cataloging-in-Publication Data

Names: Rodriguez, Tori, author. | Page, Bettie, author. | Brem, Ron, author.
Title: Bettie Page, the lost years : an intimate look at the queen
   of pinups, through her private letters & never-published photos / Tori
   Rodriguez with Ron Brem.
Description: Guilford, Connecticut : Lyons Press, [2018]
Identifiers: LCCN 2018018412 (print) | LCCN 2018018848 (ebook) | ISBN
   9781493034512 (e-book) | ISBN 9781493034505 (hardback : alk. paper)
Subjects: LCSH: Page, Bettie. | Models (Persons)—United States—Biography. |
   Page, Bettie—Correspondence. | Divorced women—California—Los
   Angeles—Biography. | Single women—California—Los Angeles—Social life
   and customs—20th century.
Classification: LCC HD6073.M772 (ebook) | LCC HD6073.M772 U5337 2018 (print)
   | DDC 746.9/2092 [B]—dc23
LC record available at https://lccn.loc.gov/2018018412

♾™ The paper used in this publication meets the minimum requirements of American National Standard for Information Sciences—Permanence of Paper for Printed Library Materials, ANSI/NISO Z39.48-1992.

Printed in the United States of America

Tori's Dedication:

This is ultimately a story about family, dedicated with endless love and appreciation to the one I'm so blessed to call mine.

Ron's Dedication:

This book has been a true labor of love. It is dedicated to my mom, Goldie, and of course to the one and only Bettie Page. To the entire world she is an icon, but to me she will always be Aunt Bettie!

Bettie Page and her mother, Edna, at Forest Park in St. Louis, Missouri, 1961.

Contents

Bettie Page and Tempest Storm in Irving Klaw's 1955 film Teaserama. Courtesy of CMG Worldwide

Foreword

I am Tempest Storm, the "Queen of Burlesque" and the last of the major stars from that glorious era when burlesque captivated audiences more than half a century ago. I am twenty-two and a half years old, having been born in Eastman, Georgia, on February 29, 1928—oh yes, that makes me a leap year baby, and like Bettie Page, we will be forever young.

Bettie and I have been linked over all these years after costarring in the 1955 Irving Klaw film *Teaserama*. Bettie was cast as my maid in the film, complete with apron. What a doll she was with that beautiful jet-black hair and those iconic U-shaped bangs. She had a perfect figure, a gorgeous smile, and a demeanor that was innocent yet sensual. We were supposed to get angry with each other during the film, and I pulled her hair in one scene. Looking back, it was really a very silly film, but somehow it became a cult classic that is still popular today.

We spent a couple of days on the set and laughed a lot, shared some meals, and talked about simple things that two young girls would chat about. Looking back, I only wish we had spent more time together and maintained contact. She was very busy becoming the most famous pinup girl in the world, and I was hitting the height of my career on stage. I became the only dancer ever to strip on the stage of Carnegie Hall—that was a highlight! And my social life was quite busy too: I dated Elvis for a year and a half and had a highly publicized romance with John F. Kennedy when he was a Massachusetts senator.

Bettie had the rare ability to express herself in so many intriguing ways once the camera was turned on. For me it is much the same—I am rather quiet and mostly a loner, but when I got on stage and the lights hit, something magical took over.

When I met my manager Harvey Robbins about a decade ago at a Bettie Page Burlesque and Doo-Wop Cruise, he insisted that I reach out to Bettie, but she was shielded by folks and I couldn't get through. I learned that she had experienced problems and was kind of isolated, and she didn't want to be seen in public after she aged. I wrote a letter and gave it to Olivia de Berardinis, the artist whose paintings of Bettie are world-renowned. She did have access to Bettie and said she read my letter to her.

Bettie passed away soon after that, in December 2008. On the day of the funeral, it actually snowed on the way to Los Angeles from Las Vegas. Hugh Hefner was in the front row with three Bunnies, and he seemed very moved. His head was down, and he hardly spoke. It was a very sad day. In my mind, I still saw Bettie smiling on set all those years ago. During the eulogy, someone read that she never quite understood all the fanfare she had received. I can understand that. Many people come up to me to this day and tell me how I have inspired them and touched their lives. I'm honored, of course, but I was only a dancer, and Bettie was—and always will be—the ultimate pinup queen.

—Tempest Storm

Introduction

When the documentary *Bettie Page Reveals All* was released in 2013, it would have been easy to assume we would never again hear directly from the adored icon who passed away in 2008. After all, the film is narrated by the Queen of Pinups herself, and she spills on lots of subjects that she had previously kept private—even in her 1996 authorized biography—though she does maintain her decades-long, no-photos rule in the movie. She was embarrassed about the weight she had gained and loathed the effects of aging—she said it made her sad to see her own celebrity idols when they were older, and wanted people to remember her as she looked in her pinup prime in the 1950s.

And there are certainly plenty of photos of Bettie from those days; in fact, she is believed to be the most photographed model of all time, with more published photos than Marilyn Monroe and Cindy Crawford combined. In addition to her own body of work, Bettie's influence shows up all over the place in pop culture as the inspiration for entertainers, artists, fashion designers, and hordes of women worldwide who idolize her.

Her enduring popularity has made her a mainstay on the *Forbes* magazine list of the world's top-earning deceased celebrities, an ongoing topic of intrigue for fans, and a muse for top stars like Madonna, Beyoncé, Katy Perry, and P!nk. But while Bettie Page the icon is firmly established, much mystery remains regarding the actual woman.

Fortunately for Bettie fans both current and to-be, a bounty of unreleased material has finally surfaced, and with it, the most intimate look yet into the life of the reclusive legend.

Found Treasures

Since well before Bettie's death from heart failure at the age of eighty-five, boxes and file folders of Bettie mementos have been gathering the clichéd dust in the closets of Bettie's nephew's house.

Ron Brem, a musician living in Bakersfield, California, is the only child of Bettie's beloved sister, Goldie Jane Page. (Bettie never had kids, other than three stepchildren during one of her four marriages to three men—she married one twice.) Like her big sis, Goldie had been an aspiring model and entertainer, even working as a burlesque dancer for a brief time in the 1950s. She hung up her pasties when she married Ron's dad in 1956, but kept up her artistic endeavors and eventually became a painting teacher and gallery owner.

In the several years before Goldie's death in the summer of 2004, she had carefully stored heaps of incredible family photos, many of which feature Bettie as either the sole subject or part of the shot. Goldie skillfully hand-colored a few of the black-and-white photos with oil pastels. None of these hundreds of photos have ever been published, and hardly anyone even knew they existed.

She also saved nearly thirty letters from Bettie spanning the years 1949 to 2000, ranging in length from one paragraph to eighteen full pages, that tell the unknown story of Bettie's "lost years" following her retirement from modeling in 1957. Most of the notes and letters were sent with a Christmas card.

As a fervent Bettie fan who has written about her for various publications, I was thrilled to meet Ron at the Viva Las Vegas Rockabilly Weekender festival in the spring of 2016. We were introduced by executives from CMG Worldwide, the company that manages the use of Bettie's image; she became a client and friend of CMG's founder, Mark Roesler, after Hugh Hefner introduced them in the '90s with the aim of getting Bettie paid for all of the products bearing her image. I work closely with CMG as the editor of Bettie's blog and official social media pages, and as an official licensee with my company, Bettie Page Fitness.

Ron showed me scans of some of the photos, and I was blown away by their beauty and specialness—and of course, honored beyond words at the opportunity to view this secret stash. He also mentioned the stack of letters from his famous aunt and said he would like to use these items for a book but was unsure of how to proceed. I recognized this rare opportunity to help tell Bettie's story through a whole different lens from anything that has been published before, and I immediately offered my assistance. I visited Ron in California later that year, where we pored over the boxes of photos and letters over a period of two days.

Letters from Bettie Page

The stories Bettie tells through these letters provide the closest look yet at her life and fill in details of what happened after she quit modeling. Some of these, of course, have never been shared, while others help to flesh out, from Bettie's personal perspective, events that have already been made public. For example, it is known that she was hospitalized for psychiatric problems on several occasions, but almost nothing has been revealed about her actual experiences during those times.

Bettie wrote some of the letters while still living with her third husband, Harry Lear, and others were penned as she served out her sentences at Patton State Psychiatric Hospital for violent altercations with landlords; she was there for twenty months the first time, and the second time she was sentenced to ten years after being found not guilty by reason of insanity. In her letters, she discusses her day-to-day doings throughout the years, her mental illness (though only using old-school euphemisms like "emotional strain" and "nervous tension") and her experiences at the hospital, as well as her hopes, regrets, struggles, and more. Excerpts from these letters are reproduced in this book uncorrected and unedited.

Never-Published Photos

Along with the letters from Bettie that fill in many gaps of her later years and further reveal the mysterious star's endearing personality, these exclusive photos span Bettie's life from infancy through 1970. Even with the photos taken during the 1950s, we've never seen this Bettie before—in scenes from her real life rather than a professional photo shoot: Bettie the sister, daughter, and aunt.

Among the countless gems in the family archives are a couple of handfuls of post-pinup photos. After she retired from modeling in 1957 and retreated into anonymity, there have been only a few published pictures of Bettie from the rest of her life, and—except for mugshots from a 1972 arrest—those later photos were taken when she was around eighty years old. While she remained resistant to having her photo taken after she gave up modeling, her former husband snapped her in 1958, and Goldie got some shots during a couple of family gatherings in the 1960s and '70s.

Other rarities include a photo of Bettie as a baby, shots of her parents and siblings, her first modeling composite card from the 1940s, never-seen photos of Bettie during the pinup days, and more. There are also some gorgeous solo images of Goldie, a stunning beauty in her own right who looked a lot like Bettie.

The photos of Bettie and Goldie together are especially compelling. One set from the early 1950s, for example, features the sisters on the beach at Coney Island. Even when they're striking a pose, the images retain a touching candor and innocence, since they are not professional photos. In a lot of these shots, the sisters are wearing bikinis they made by hand—at a time when it was basically unheard of and quite scandalous for women to wear bikinis in public.

Other neat mementos include poems from Goldie's diary that outline key events in Bettie's and her family's life, and letters exchanged between Goldie and their brother Jack in the early '90s in which they discuss Bettie's newfound fame.

Bettie has become a symbol of authenticity, sexual freedom, and unabashed nudity. She rejected the notion that nudity is immoral or sinful, once saying, "I want to be remembered as the woman who changed people's perspectives concerning nudity in its natural form." Ironically, this new part of her story—told in her own words to her family as the events unfolded—may be the barest we will ever see the beloved pinup queen.

First modeling composite, San Francisco, 1945.

PART I
The Early Years

The trailblazing woman who was destined to become the eternally reigning pinup queen was born on April 22, 1923, in Nashville, Tennessee, to Edna and Roy Page. Her given name was Betty Mae Page, though she later changed the spelling of her first name to "Bettie," and that's the version that stuck. She was the second of six children that included three brothers and two sisters, including Goldie, with whom Bettie remained close throughout their lives.

Their childhood was marked by extreme poverty, instability, and sexual abuse by their father, who was also a notorious womanizer and

In a photo from 1923, Walter Roy Page holds Bettie on the right and Billy on the left.

once spent two years in prison for stealing a car. During that time, their mother could no longer afford to take care of all the children without Roy's support, so when Bettie was ten years old, Edna sent the three girls to live in an orphanage for at least a year—where Bettie recalled that dinner was always a piece of plain white cake and a cup of milk.

While there, the sisters would practice modeling poses together that they had seen in the newspaper and magazines. In a 1998 interview with *Playboy*, Bettie said those practice sessions marked the start of her modeling career. Both Goldie and Bettie aspired to be entertainers.

A modeling photo of Bettie from 1946.

Goldie in 1947.

*Bettie and Goldie,
date unknown, but
Bettie is probably
about sixteen years old.*

Despite the abusive and chaotic home life, frequent hunger, and various other struggles, Bettie made exemplary grades at the prestigious Hume-Fogg High School, where she was a fixture on the honor roll for all four of her years there. She kept busy with a full plate of extracurricular activities, too: In her yearbook, a few of her many credits include coeditor of the school newspaper, secretary and treasurer of the student council, member of the drama club and the debate club, and Girl Most Likely to Succeed for two years in a row.

High school days, around 1940. From left to right: Joyce, Jimmie, Bettie, and Goldie.

Christmas at the Parthenon in Nashville, Tennessee, in 1944. L–R: Jimmie, Bettie, Goldie, and Jack.

Bettie was devastated when she lost the chance—by a fraction of a point!—to be valedictorian of her class and thereby win a full scholarship to Vanderbilt University. Instead, she was awarded salutatorian and received a small scholarship to Peabody College, which has since merged with Vanderbilt. Working as a secretary for a Civil War novelist to cover her remaining school costs, she earned a bachelor's degree in teaching, but she quickly realized it wasn't the right career path for her—she thought it was too difficult to corral the students, especially the boys.

While still in college, Bettie married Billy Neal, who had been her classmate in high school. When he was drafted into the navy during World War II, the couple moved to San Francisco. The marriage was short-lived—largely due to his jealousy, according to Bettie—and they divorced in 1947. (They remarried in the 1960s, but that stint was short-lived too.) In 1949 she moved to New

Early modeling photos, San Francisco, 1946.

York City, where she got her own apartment and worked as a secretary while modeling and taking acting classes.

In November of that year, Bettie wrote a note inside a birthday card she sent to Goldie (using three one-cent stamps!), who was living in San Francisco at the time.

1949, November—New York City

"Hi! After so long a time, I hardly know what to say!" she starts. "Hope you're feeling ship-shape and still giving the sailors a whirl." About hearing from their brother Jimmie that Goldie had mentioned wanting to get married, Bettie cautions, "Luck to you, but be sure that's what you really want now. Don't be like me and get talked into something you weren't ready for—meaning marriage."

She talks about still seeing first husband Billy Neal periodically, including during his recent one-month stay with her in New York City. "Someday, when I decide I really want to be a wife, we'll probably get married again," she says. "I've dated oodles of other fellows but somehow can't get interested in anybody but Billy—it's a funny thing, but true.

"As you may know, I'm doing photographic and fashion modeling with Pat Allen agency right now," she wrote, and she mentions a recent off-Broadway part. "The competition in N.Y. is terrific but I enjoy the show business life— except for the gorillas. . . . It's 100 times more interesting than secretarial work." She especially liked that she could make the same amount of money modeling for two hours that she would make from a full week at her desk job.

Bettie and Joyce in 1949.

Goldie, Edna, and Bettie, date unknown.

Goldie in New York.

In a glimpse of the sweet encouragement she offered Goldie at several points in the letters over the years, Bettie asks, "Are you doing anything with your drawing, or do you still say you're not good enough? I know better.

"If you ever feel like a change of scenery, why don't you come to New York and stay with me? I have a big housekeeping one-room apartment convenient to everything." Goldie took her up on her offer, and it is during these visits that the sisters casually modeled for a few sets of beautiful photos on the beach at Coney Island and elsewhere.

"Write me all the gossip whenever you get in the mood, hear? I'm the world's worst correspondent, but I'll answer eventually. Bettie," she closes, then adds, "P.S. I like your new name." Goldie had legally changed her name to Gloria because she didn't think her given name fit her, according to Ron.

Not long after her arrival in New York City, Bettie survived a horrifying sexual assault by five men, which was depicted in the unauthorized film *The Notorious Bettie Page,* and which Bettie herself later described in *Bettie Page Reveals All.* Somehow, she managed to forge ahead in pursuing her ultimate goal of movie stardom. Bettie was a major movie buff, and her true desire was to be an actress, and while she did have a few close opportunities, that dream never materialized. (In a 1998 interview, she cited the failed acting career and her inability to have children as her major regrets.)

However, Bettie's unplanned path to pinup queendom would soon emerge after a chance encounter on the beach.

Bettie and Goldie photographed at the beach in 1951.

PART II
The Pinup Years

B ettie was walking along the beach on Coney Island in 1950 when she met Jerry Tibbs, an African-American police officer who was also an amateur photographer. He suggested that she cut bangs into her hairstyle to balance her high forehead, and he helped her create her first pinup modeling portfolio. She was soon posing frequently at camera club shoots and ultimately worked with several notable photographers, including jazz bandleader Cass Carr, crime and street photographer Weegee, famed fetish photographer Irving Klaw, silent film star Harold Lloyd, and pinup-turned-photographer Bunny Yeager.

Her work with Yeager produced some of her most popular shots, one of which ended up in an early issue of *Playboy* magazine. In the January 1955 issue, Bettie became one of the recently launched publication's first centerfolds, with the well-known pose of her nude and winking as she hangs an ornament on a Christmas tree.

She also appeared in a long list of other men's magazines and a few for sports and outdoors enthusiasts. (Goldie left a stack of these to Ron Brem; she would buy them if she could afford them when she spotted them in stores.) Bettie once sought representation from the Ford modeling agency but was rejected for being too voluptuous.

During the '50s, it's hard to believe she did anything but work nonstop, considering the countless photos that were taken of her in that short span of time. However, she did carve out space in her schedule for two of her favorite leisure activities, dancing and exercising, as well as occasional dating. One of the men she had a relationship with was the renowned car designer Richard Arbib. He later gushed about her in *Bettie Page Reveals All*, and it's clear that he saw her as "the one that got away." Howard Hughes reportedly asked her out, but she turned down the invitation.

Bettie also made time to hand-sew many of her costumes, typically bikinis and lingerie that were extremely risqué by that era's standards. Her creations were so appealing and unique that a catalog company tricked her into modeling for them so they could steal her designs—and use her photos to sell the products.

Bettie called it quits on her modeling work in 1957 and abruptly vanished from public view. She later said it was because she was getting too old to model at age thirty-four, and she thought there were so many photos of her that people must have been tired of seeing her. One of the main reasons often cited for her departure from the business, however, was the investigation into Irving Klaw's fetish and bondage photography business, which sold the then-scandalous photos through catalogs to private clients and under the counters of various shops. When Senator Estes Kefauver, who was the Democratic nominee in the 1952 presidential election, spearheaded a campaign against "indecency" as part of his platform, Klaw became one of his main targets.

Bettie was subpoenaed to appear at the trial but was never called to testify, though FBI agents showed up at her apartment to intimidate her with folders of her nude photos—which were considered pornographic and were illegal to sell back then, even if they were mild by any reasonable standard. It has been said that the experience with the Feds was a key factor that turned her off modeling.

As the repression of the 1950s yielded to the liberation of the next decade, Bettie's joyful sexuality and shameless nudity made her a symbol of sexual liberation. It has been widely proclaimed that she inadvertently paved the way for the sexual revolution of the 1960s when many Americans began vehemently resisting Kefauver-style oppression.

Pinup Gallery: Bettie and Goldie in New York and Miami, 1951

Most of the modeling shots in this gallery were shot at Coney Island. The less formal shots were taken in New York and Miami. The photographers are unknown. Although Bettie and Goldie looked very much alike, Bettie could be distinguished from her sister by her trademark bangs.

Bettie in St. Petersburg, Florida, in 1958. Photo taken by then-husband Armon Walterson.

PART III
The Lost Years

By the time the movements for women's liberation and sexual freedom were ramping up, though, Bettie was already worlds away from her pinup days. For the first couple of years following her retirement from modeling, Bettie was in an incompatible, lackluster marriage with the twelve-years-younger Armon Walterson (whom she had previously dated) beginning in 1958. (Although his name is most often spelled "Armond," it was actually Armon, as shown on genealogy records and in Bettie's spelling on photo captions shown within this book.)

While residing with Armon in Key West, Florida, Bettie briefly taught

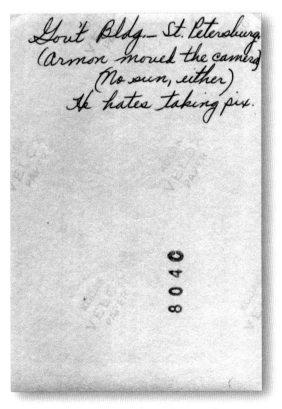

Bettie's notes on the back of the adjacent photo.

elementary school but said she gave it up after becoming too flustered with rowdy students. She became a born-again Christian on New Year's Eve 1959, and she and Armon grew even further apart. Though the couple divorced in 1963, she left him well before that and attended several Bible schools and retreats in different parts of the country, including Los Angeles, Chicago, and Portland.

Armon in the Everglades in 1958.

Bettie has also said that she worked as a counselor for the Billy Graham Crusades, stating in an interview, "If ever there is a man of God it is Billy Graham. . . . I admire the man very much." After the 1949 note to Goldie that Bettie wrote at the start of her modeling career, we next hear from her in August 1962. (As Ron noted wryly, "Bettie was pretty busy during the '50s.") That note was written on a postcard sent from a Billy Graham Bible conference.

She was so passionate about her religious commitment that she applied to become a Christian missionary but was rejected because she had already been divorced. In hopes of remedying that problem, she went back to Nashville and remarried Billy Neal—just as predicted in her 1949 letter to Goldie—in 1963, as soon as her divorce from Armon was finalized. However, they quickly divorced again.

The second letter from the 1960s was written while Bettie was back in Nashville working toward a master's degree in English. She never finished her degree and instead returned to Florida, where she met her third husband, Harry Lear, while out dancing one night. The two were married from 1967 to 1972. It was during this time that she had her first known psychotic break, and it is just after their divorce (and a stay in the hospital) that her letters resume again and become fairly steady through the year 2000.

Letters from Bettie: Dispatches from the Lost Years

THE 1960S

1962, August—Winona Lake, Indiana

Bettie sent this postcard from the Billy Sunday Tabernacle—"Home of the World's Greatest Bible Conference"—in Winona Lake, Indiana. She would sometimes send correspondence to one family member and ask to have it sent along to the others. This letter is addressed to her mother: "Dear Mama, Hi! Haven't heard from you in so long—hope my last letter didn't cause any hard feelings. We've had too many of those in the Page family—ha!"

At the time of this letter, she had left Armon a couple of years earlier and was immersed in her Bible studies. She describes being happily busy with the Billy Graham Crusades and learning from some of the best Bible teachers in the country. (Steve Brewster, the founder of the fan club The Bettie Scouts and personal friend to Bettie in her older years, said she was one of the sharpest, best-informed Bible scholars he's ever known.)

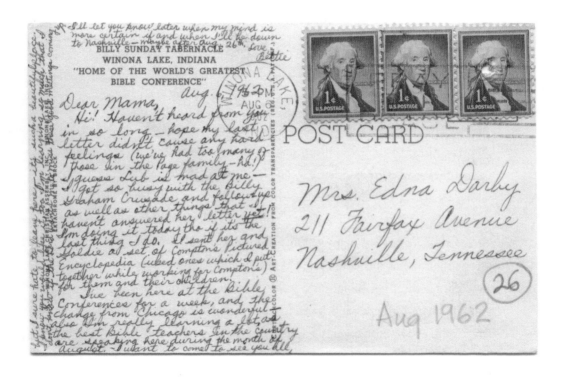

*Postcard from the Billy Sunday Tabernacle in Winona Lake, Indiana,
where Bettie took Bible classes in the summer of 1962.*

She goes on to mention that she wants to visit the family in Nashville, but "I'm learning so much that I don't know if the Lord wants me to miss these good meetings coming up."

Bettie, Edna, Ron, and Goldie at home in Illinois in 1961. It's hard to believe that by this time Bettie had retired from modeling.

Bettie in Nashville in 1964 with her father (in car), his girlfriend, Ron Brem's dad, and an unknown man.

1965, December—Nashville, Tennessee

When she sent this Christmas card to Goldie and her husband and son, Bettie was living with her mother in Nashville, pursuing her master's degree, and teaching Sunday school. She had enrolled again at her alma mater, Peabody College for Teachers. As evident in the excerpt below, things are sounding grim but she remains optimistic:

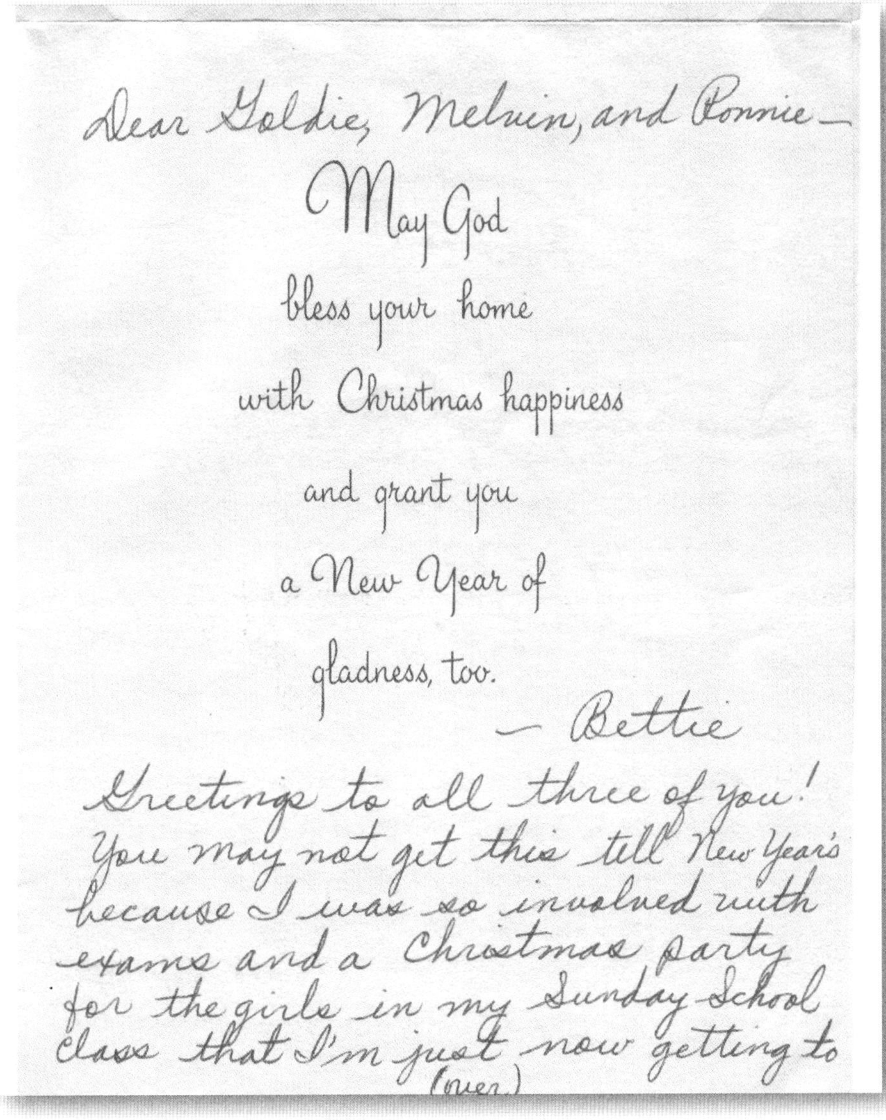

Dear Goldie, Melvin, and Ronnie—

May God
bless your home
with Christmas happiness
and grant you
a New Year of
gladness, too.
— Bettie

Greetings to all three of you! You may not get this till New Year's because I was so involved with exams and a Christmas party for the girls in my Sunday School class that I'm just now getting to
(over)

−2−

write a few notes and mail cards. Please forgive us for not sending you all a gift. Mama and I are both flat financially at the moment, and I'm going to have to get her a little present by charging it to her Sears-Roebuck account and paying it later. With the few bucks I had, I bought a "$1.00" present for each of my 13-yr. girls" at the church (most of them are poorer than we were at that age) so they would have a merrier Christmas. It made me feel real good inside to do it, and I am beginning to understand what the Lord means by "It's more blessed to give than to receive," especially when you're helping somebody who really needs it. I'm going to do something like this every Christmas if I'm able.

Mama and I are both flat financially at the moment, and I'm going to have to get her a little present by charging it to her Sears-Roebuck account and paying it later. With the few bucks I had I bought a $1.00 present for each of my 13-yr. [old] girls at the church (most of them are poorer than we were at that age) so they would have a merrier Christmas. It made me feel real good inside to do it, and I am beginning to understand what the

Lord means by "It is more blessed to give than to receive," especially when you're helping someone who really needs it. I'm going to do something like this every Christmas if I'm able.

She talks about how much harder academia is for her this time around, and says she's already worn out.

It seems to be the Lord's will that I get my Master's Degree at Peabody and plan to teach. He has gotten me two loans and a scholarship which will enable me to make it till June 1st if I don't collapse from the strain of too much studying. It is twice as hard to get a Master's as a Bachelor's. They expect you to be a genius and be able to read a big thick book in a couple of hours and remember everything you read. I'm already exhausted, and I have three more quarters (winter, spring, and summer) to go! You know, I'm beginning to realize something—your brain and eyes get tired of studying as you get older, in addition to everything else.

Adding to her stress was her mother's instability: "This business of getting old has really got Mama whipped. She is very depressed and seems to be trying to drink herself to death. Every penny she gets goes to liquor." Bettie says that living in that environment is "such a terrible strain that I can't concentrate on my lessons and get the rest and peace of mind necessary to go to school."

Her other sister, who was nicknamed "Lub," and her four daughters had visited during the Thanksgiving that had just passed. Bettie describes the girls to Goldie, noting how pretty and smart they are and how much she likes them. "We played a game of acting out imaginary play scenes (which I dreamed up) for hours and judging who did the best job of it. Also, they sang and did readings on my tape recorder," she recalls.

"When are you coming for another visit? . . . Let us know how you are & what Ronnie got from Santa. Love, Bettie"

THE 1970S

Edna's sixty-ninth birthday in 1970. From left to right:
Jimmie, Edna, Billie, Goldie, Bettie, and Jack.

1973, December—Miami Springs, Florida

By this point, Bettie and Harry had married and divorced, but he is still allowing her to live in a room in his house "out of the goodness of his big generous heart," she says in this Christmas card to Goldie; her husband, Mel; and Ron. "I don't know what I would do without Harry's help. It has really been a Godsend." (In later interviews, she said they had a good marriage but that it was pretty quickly ruined by his ex-wife's constant harassing of Bettie, Harry's handling of which led Bettie to call him a "Mr. Milquetoast.")

Hi! Hope you all are well and kicking all over the place. Thank you, Gloria, for that nice long letter you sent me while I was in the hospital. My nerves were really acting up then. I would have liked very much to spend a week or so with you at Mama's but I don't have any money. I've been getting my groceries out of the $50.00 Harry gives me monthly for alimony. He's just letting me have this room (which used to be Pop's room) in the back of the house out of the goodness of his big generous heart. I don't know what I would do without Harry's help. It has really been a Godsend. At the time you wrote me, I couldn't even write. I have had a bad form of arthritis called capsilitis of the shoulder. I'm just now beginning to use my right arm. I couldn't even sleep on it for months. I still can't fasten a bra or zip anything in the back; just can't get my arm back there.

I hope you are not freezing up there. We're getting some cold weather down here, too. Last night it was 40 degrees. I have an air conditioner in here but it doesn't heat up the place much and it sounds like a cyclone.

Gloria, I hope you and Melvin and Ronnie will have the nicest Christmas you've ever had and the best new year ever.

I love all of you,
Bettie

She thanks Goldie for a long letter she sent while Bettie was in the hospital. She had been arrested in October 1972 after threatening Harry and his three kids with a butcher knife, warning that she would cut their guts out if they stopped staring at a picture of Jesus hanging on the wall. She recalled, "My nerves were really acting up then." This is the first of several euphemisms we'll see Bettie use that are typical of the way people would describe symptoms of mental illness decades ago—even psychotic disorders like schizophrenia—since the stigma and shame associated with it were even worse back then than they are now.

Again, she wishes she could visit but doesn't have any money; she buys groceries with the fifty dollars in monthly alimony from Harry.

Bettie mentions that she has a form of arthritis called capsulitis of the shoulder, a painful condition also known as "frozen shoulder," one of many ailments she will mention over the next several decades.

"Gloria, I hope you and Melvin and Ronnie will have the nicest Christmas you've ever had and the best new year ever. I love all of you, Bettie."

1974, December—Miami Springs, Florida

Bettie thanks Goldie and Ron for a poem about springtime that they composed and sent with their last letter to her. Presumably in response to something in that poem or letter, Bettie says, "No, I don't have any cute little rabbits hopping about, but I do have some blue jays, mockingbirds, an oriole, and oodles of sparrows which I feed. I like to watch them through Harry's binoculars."

Then she shares the bad news:

> *I'm not doing too good these days. I've had a lot of trouble with bursitis, calcium deposits, and arthritis in my shoulders and hips, but the worst thing is my nerves. Every few days I have a nervous bout for no apparent reason. I can't even go to work. I just don't understand what's happening to me. I'm just falling apart.*

She again expresses her gratitude to Harry, who is still taking care of her. She also mentions that the previous summer, she was hospitalized for five weeks "battling emotional strain." There's another old-school euphemism for a psychotic break.

1975, December—Miami Springs, Florida

"Greetings and all that thar jazz!" the note begins. "I wish we could all be together this Christmas. If only I were a thousandaire!" She lauds "Ronnie," as they called Ron back then, for playing in a band, and mentions that she is taking weekly piano lessons at Miami Springs High School via their adult education courses. She had been searching for a job with no luck thus far: "It's a shame that I can't teach, but the nervous strain of it would be too much for me. I'm afraid to try it."

As in several of her letters, she details her various pets and birds she feeds with bird feeders in her yard, as well as the types of flowers and plants in her surroundings. In this one, she says, "My thirty sparrows, ten doves, three blue jays, two cardinals, one mockingbird, and one red-headed woodpecker all wish you a merry Christmas." With the bird feeder mounted just outside her back door, "I can stand behind the glass jalousies and watch them (just six feet away) splashing in the bird bath and eating. They all hang out in the bougainvillea and hibiscus bushes just behind the feeder."

She is still living with Harry and talks about how her former stepchildren are doing. About the oldest, she writes, "Larry is really a nice boy. In January he will begin his third year of college as a psychology major."

Bettie was painting her room at the time—light green and white—and complains about how sore it makes her muscles and wrists. "The old gray mare just ain't what she used to be," she laments before signing off.

"Be good to yourselves, and have a happy holiday season. Little Poe (our cute little white toy poodle) says hello to you all. Bettie."

1977, August—Miami Springs, Florida
(Letter addressed first to Bettie's brother Jimmie and then sent to Goldie)

Bettie had finally found work as a temp and said she would have to keep her "fingers tied to the secretarial grindstone" for a while in order to get some repairs on the 1967 blue Mustang Harry had bought her so she could get around to her temporary job assignments, and she was glad it didn't come with any debt attached:

> *I don't have to pay Harry back either (thank the Lord) because we both feel he owed it to me since he drove my Falcon for over five years—he gave Pat his good car when they were divorced—and his old one went on the blink shortly after we were married; without my car he would have had to buy himself another one long before he did.*

She goes into quite a bit of technical detail about the car parts needing repair "in order to get it in as tip-toppy condition as possible for its age," including "two new universal joints and some bushings (whatever those are)." She had just signed up for an auto mechanic course for women called "Know Your Car," with the aim of saving money on routine maintenance: "I should have taken a course like that many years ago, but better late than never!" She had also checked out four books on car repair from the library and was "studying them like mad in my spare time."

The Dewhurst brothers who run the garage nearby also gave her tips on how to keep the car in shape:

> *They say if I change the oil and the oil filter every 3,000 miles (like Jack told me) and attend to the transmission fluid, the power steering reservoir, the radiator water, the battery water, and the rear axle lubrication regularly—plus bringing the car in for an engine tune-up every 10,000 miles*

*(which includes changing the carburetor air fil-
ter) and whenever I hear any unusual sound in
the motor—I can keep my 10-year-old Mustang
running for 130,000 miles or more just like the
Dewhurst brothers do with their cars. My car has
a total of 72,000 miles on it altogether, so if I keep
it in good operating condition and don't run it
over 50 miles an hour on the Expressways, maybe
I won't have to invest in another car for a while.*

Bettie wishes she could head to Nashville to join the rest of the family for her mother's upcoming birthday, but again has no money to spare, this time because she will need to move out on her own soon when Harry sells the house for a job transfer out of state.

She says, "Jimmie, I phoned Goldie (I just can't get used to calling her Gloria) this morning and talked to her for about fifteen minutes." Goldie had just gotten divorced, and the sisters had explored the idea of getting an apartment together in Florida or elsewhere:

*We also discussed the possibility of going out to
California and getting a place to live near you (so
she and I could fall in the creek again on the way
to Griffith Park while horseback riding; do you
remember that? On second thought, Goldie is the
only one who got dunked in the creek while her
horse went trotting back to the stables).*

She urges Jimmie to take it easy on Goldie during an upcoming visit, asking him to remember that not everyone is "able to pull out from under great per-sonal losses and disappointments with the same mental and physical strength that you have. Whether you believe it or not, it's still true that we're not all the same emotionally and we don't all react to terrible stress and strain in the same way. (End of lecture.)"

When describing where she might like to live next, Bettie says, "The only problem might be the landladys." Though she was referencing whether she would be able to bring her poodle with her to her next place of residence, this statement could have made for some strong foreshadowing if this were a work of fiction. "I say landlady because I would prefer to get an efficiency apartment attached to the house of a private family rather than an impersonal apartment building where all kinds of meanness imaginable goes on here in Miami."

Further exploring her options, she says, "Or I may sell my furniture (except the piano), ship my belongings American Express, hop in my little ole jalopy—after I get a few hundred of those green rectangles sticking to my fingers—and head for California!" Although her mom and two of her brothers were still in Nashville, moving back there wasn't an appealing option for Bettie because she'd gotten used to being out of the cold:

> *I probably would if the weather was warm all year round and the trees stayed green and the flowers bloomed all the time and you could go to the beach whenever you wanted to; these things I've grown accustomed to and these things I like (as long as I have a choice). I might even end up in Hawaii; I've always wanted to go there. Say, maybe you and Goldie might go with me to Waikiki, who knows?*

Bettie ends the letter with well wishes to Jimmie for his trip to Nashville. "Have a nice time in Opryland (I watch <u>Hee-Haw</u> occasionally, even if the jokes are the corniest yet)."

1978, April—Miami Springs, Florida

(Letter addressed to Bettie's mom and siblings; she sent them each a copy.)

"Sorry it's been 'long time, no hear' from me as usual, but how many of you are known for being faithful letter writers? (Ha!)" the greeting goes. The next statement should serve as a reminder that the invention of e-mail was a godsend: "Please forgive this crummy paper, lousy carbon paper, and error-filled typing, but it's the best I can offer at the moment. I don't feel like writing a separate letter to each one of you; this is the only way I can produce five copies at one whack; hope you can read 'em."

A bit later in the letter: "Unfortunately, the 54 years of mind and emotional tension-strains that has been my lot (coupled with the aging process) periodically, that is, are taking their toll on my poor little old body. . . . To put it bluntly, I think I came very close to kicking the bucket two weeks ago from a heart attack." Over a period of several days, she experienced lots of

scary sensations resembling heart problems, which became more numerous and frequent until she thought she "was just about to go down in the valley of the shadow of the you-know-what with the Lord." She describes the symptoms that have been plaguing her for the past two months:

> *Severe and prolonged indigestion; all kinds of weird chest pains and strange goings-on in my chest and left arm; heavy pressure on my chest like somebody standing on it if I do any housekeeping or cooking, etc., or exert myself physically in any way for as much as an hour or so; blood rushing all over my body or something causing ten-hot-flashes-in-one, leaving me soaking wet and burning up, which is so frightening that I can't explain it . . . when this happens, my heart begins to thump real loud and, beating like a trip-hammer afterwards, it scares me half to death—when one of these compounded hot blood racings, to my face and chest mostly, is over, I can't even feel any heartbeat when I take my pulse or I can just barely feel light irregular*

beats, not at all what my usual heartbeat sounds like.

In a panic during a recurrent episode of these symptoms, she finally called the rescue squad at the fire station—whose frenzied activity clearly did little to ease her fears!

> *It was just like the TV show EMERGENCY. They came rushing in the front door with an ambulance waiting outside and the police sirens blaring; one fellow began testing my heart with an EKG while another guy pushed an oxygen cup in front of my face and told me to breathe into it; then a third man started setting up an I.V. in a hurry like they do on television—you know, the bottle of salt solution with a long cord attached to it and a huge needle stuck in my arm for over five hours; they set me in some kind of special chair and carried me downstairs to the ambulance lickety-split and away we went ninety miles an hour to the nearest hospital emergency room. Boy, the way they were acting I thought I had had it for sure! I expected to have an excruciating heart attack any minute.*

At the hospital, the ER doctors ran an EKG and other tests, which revealed no issues with her heart. However, the symptoms had not diminished, so she was scheduled to see a cardiologist for further examination. "Maybe it's only aftereffects of the nervous strains I've had several times during the past six years coupled with the menopause (which the doctors say I'm still in)," she suggested. "Whatever it is, I've got to find out so something can be done about it, if possible."

According to Bettie, Harry will be moving to South Carolina in ten days and she will stay in the apartment a bit longer. With the uncertainty about long-term living arrangements, she had given up her beloved pet Poe to Harry's mother in Pennsylvania.

She says Harry and his soon-to-be-wife June want to eventually buy a small farm and have Bettie live there and take care of the garden and animals.

"Imagine that: Harry's wife and his ex-wife helping him run a farm!" she writes. "June is a very unusual woman. I don't think she has a jealous bone in her body. I like her very much and believe she will be a good wife for Harry."

Meanwhile, Bettie is dating a building contractor named Michael there in Florida, and he and his brothers want her to move to their property so they can take care of her:

> *Michael lives with three of his brothers (there are seven of them altogether; they said their parents tried for many years to have a girl, but finally gave up after Baby Boy No. 7 arrived—that's a nickname for the youngest). They also call him Beebee Seven, which I think is very cute and original. When their mother and father died several years ago, all of the Siegfried brothers joined together to run the family business (they're building contractors); they take on construction projects all over the state of Florida—that's the only thing I don't like: Michael is away from the Miami area a lot. He just came back from a two-month job in Tallahassee helping to put up a four-story office building.*

Michael and his brothers have a large house with maintenance workers living on site, so Bettie would have help nearby if an emergency arose. It is implied that he wants to marry her, though it's not explicitly stated:

> *Since my health has taken a turn for the worse, I'm in no position to even think of getting married at this time; besides, I haven't known Michael very long, and maybe I'm getting cold feet at the very thought of taking the plunge again. Of course, women do change their minds, you know—and who knows what the future may bring?*

She apologizes for sounding morbid and going into such detail about her ailments, but wanted to keep them informed in case something should happen to her—"Heaven forbid! That would be <u>some</u> birthday present, wouldn't it?

(Oops, pardon me, I don't even want to think of April 22nd anymore—in fact, I've decided it's not on the calendar from this day forward).

"Be good to yourselves, all of you, and let me know what you're up to whenever any juicy or non-juicy newsy tidbits of interest occur. Harry says 'Hello' and so does Poe from Pennsylvania (I'm sure). Love, Bettie"

1978, November—Lawndale, California

By this point Bettie had made up her mind about where to live next, and she had moved from Florida to California to live with her brother Jimmie the month before she wrote this letter. Similar to several of the others over the years, this one starts with, "Dear Mama, I hope you're not mad at me because I haven't written to you much lately or come to see you, but I've had so many money problems and body and mind problems that I've had a hard time adjusting to all of it."

She had wanted to go to Nashville on the way to Jimmie's, but "I was short on that green stuff and wouldn't have had enough to help out with my food bill while I was there; so I just took the cheapest southern Greyhound bus route to Los Angeles. I would have been too much of a burden on you anyway."

She feels that Jimmie is mistreating her, and she rants about him for the better part of this thirteen-page letter, detailing what amounts to ongoing verbal abuse. He's always irritable and critical of everything Bettie does, including the noise she makes when preparing dinner for the two of them, or even just talking.

Unhappily, I've found out from personal experience that Jimmie does not treat anyone with <u>kindness</u> except strangers!! And the worst part of it is this: he seems to enjoy picking on people's faults and telling them to their faces what he doesn't like about them. I remember he used to do that years ago, but I thought as he got older (and supposedly wiser) that he had outgrown that <u>obnoxious habit</u>. But he's worse about it now than ever! He won't even let me talk to him; he says I never "have anything <u>important</u> to say and everything I say is 'gobbledy-gook,' as he calls it. (You can imagine how I feel when he tells me that!) Even if I have to

Bettie Page
14223 FIRMONA AVE
LAWNDALE CALIF 90260

tuesday,
Nov. 21st
1978

Dear Mama,

I hope you're not mad at me because I haven't written to you much lately or come to see you, but I've had so many money problems and body and mind problems that I've had a hard time adjusting to all of it. I wanted to come up to Nashville to see you on the way to California but I was short on that green stuff and wouldn't have had enough to help out with my food bill while I was there; so I just took the cheapest southern Grey-hound bus route to Los Angeles. I would have been too much of a burden on you anyway.

I'm sending you a Thanksgiving card with this letter but you won't get 'em till some time after Thanksgiving because I fouled up my good intentions by spending so much time and effort writing a 25 or 30 page letter to Jack; when I started on it I was just going to write a few pages, <u>but I've been</u>

needing to talk to someone (about my troubles with Jimmie) so badly that I just kept writing on the letter every few hours for three or four days — and I didn't get my cards and letters off to you and Harry and June before it was too late for you to receive them by Thanksgiving. But I'm going ahead and sending the cards anyway. Please forgive me — late Bettie as usual (ha!). I asked Jack to bring the longwinded letter to you and let you read it so you would know how things are going with Jimmie and me (not sohot, unfortunately), and I wouldn't have to write it all again to you. Maybe you or Jack could send it on to Goldie to read. I don't know if she is planning to come to California, expecting to stay with Jimmie for awhile. If she is, she should know that Jimmie has got his own emotional hangups and is full of bitterness (apparently towards everybody) because of the disappointments and failures in his life; he is not *ask him a question that needs to be answered, <u>he</u> <u>interrupts</u> and <u>starts talking right on top of what</u> <u>I'm saying</u>, or he tells me to "<u>shut up and leave me</u> <u>alone</u>," or he turns up the TV louder so he can't hear me <u>even if it's during a commercial</u>, or <u>he</u> <u>takes off out the door fuming</u> because I'm bothering him. (I've been trying to get him to eat better food so maybe it would improve his disposition as well as his nerves)—<u>he won't listen with any kind of</u> <u>courtesy to a word I say, but he expects me to listen</u> <u>to every word he says</u>. Oh, you'd better believe he expects that! Also, Jimmie thinks he has the right to criticize everything about me and everything I do, but I'm not supposed to criticize <u>him</u> about anything. Oh no! <u>He thinks he's perfect in every</u> <u>way</u> and I'm just too dumb and unintelligent (as he keeps telling me) for him to waste his time on.*

She pauses to rein in it, saying she shouldn't get started on those complaints—and then continues:

But I must not get started on the way I feel because of the <u>ugly, hateful attitudes</u> Jimmie has had towards me from the moment I got here. <u>I should</u> <u>not have come to Jimmie's house in the first place</u>; we have very little privacy from each other. If I make any noise at all, it annoys him. <u>When he</u> <u>comes home from work I have to practically stop</u> <u>living</u>! He starts watching football on television every day as soon as he gets in the door, or something else on TV—and <u>if I even say anything to</u> <u>him or make a sound</u>, he starts ranting and raving like a mad man. But I have to make <u>some noise</u> making supper for us, even he knows that! In order to be as quiet as possible and not disturb his TV watching, I started leaving the dishes in the sink

Bettie's still living at his old address and reports that her job search isn't going so well, so she "may have to assemble electronic parts or something like that in one of these factories—with much lower pay—in order to eat and pay the rent." The landlady had told her she wouldn't raise the rent even though rental prices in the area had increased substantially in recent years.

In the one outing she and Jimmie did have together during this time, they took the two-and-a-half-hour bus ride to the Hollywood Christmas Parade. Bettie mentions that there were more than forty TV and movie stars in it, and she thoroughly enjoyed it. It's ironic to think of this anonymous icon watching the stars go by, literally parading past her while living out her long-lost dream, no less.

She isn't sure if she wants to stay in California because it's not the same as when she went to Bible school in LA in 1960 and 1961: "It used to be nice and warm all year; now it is in the 40s every night all winter!" She has been miserably cold without heat in her bedroom or bathroom, and she's caught several colds in the short time she's been there. "Over half of the people have bronchial troubles of some kind because the smog is so terrible. It hangs over this entire valley so thick you can't even see 50 feet in front of you sometimes."

Those often-intersecting issues of aging and ailing figure prominently again in this letter:

> I guess we're beginning to get old and our health is going to pot along with it. I've been falling apart more and more the last few years. The thought of being alone in ill health with no money is beginning to frighten me, as I am sure you must be feeling the same way. I would like to get married again (if I can find someone who is compatible with me and will have me—ha!). At our ages it is not easy; as you no doubt have discovered, these men want spring chickens, not old hens. I would like to go dancing again (not this disco-rock stuff—I mean beautiful ballroom dancing), but my shoulders, legs, and ankles are so full of bursitis, tendonitis, and arthritis (you name it and I've got it), etc., that I don't know if I'm able to do it anymore. That makes me sad. Maybe I'll have to

be content just dancing by myself to the FM radio (which I do for short periods of time without this stinking arthritis bothering me too much). . . . As Mama says, "Oh, to be young again!" But moaning and fretting over that spilled milk is <u>not</u> going to help—it only makes matters worse.

She mentions that she's gotten more into positive thinking and had recently bought three longevity and positive-thinking books, including one by Norman Vincent Peale, author of *The Power of Positive Thinking*, which have been helping her cope.

It is helping me very much to read the good advice in these books; maybe you would like to get copies of them, too. When I get my tape recorder fixed (it's on the blink), I'm going to put certain parts of these books on tape and play it over and over again until it comes out my ears. <u>I need it</u> right now! When Jimmie was fussing at me over everything I said and did, two things helped me tremendously to take it without blowing my cork too much: <u>praying to the Lord</u> and repeating to myself over and over, "<u>I will remain calm and peaceful right now.</u>" It's hard to do when someone is running you down, belittling you, criticizing you, and picking you to pieces every time you open your mouth (like Jimmie does me), but it works if you can do it. Of course, the best thing is to get as far away from such problems as you can. I would have moved away from Jimmie within a week after I got here from Miami if I had had enough money. My nerves were really shot almost by the time he got another place to stay. I've been recuperating from it during the past two weeks, and I feel much better.

Later in the letter she talks about being flat broke and that she may have to borrow money from someone if she can't find a job soon. "I'm having a hard time being on my own again without the financial security and companion-ship" of marriage. Herein lies the sweetness of Bettie: On one page she's talking about positive thinking, and on the next she's talking about being flat broke and burdened with physical ailments. This is who she was; she didn't see that those things might be contradictory, and she likely wouldn't have cared.

She mentions that perhaps she'll move to Hawaii or back to Florida, and then suggests that maybe Goldie move to California and they could live together or near each other: "Maybe we could help each other Gloria (I will get used to call-ing you that; it does suit you better than Goldie; Gloria is a very pretty name)." Thirty years into Goldie's name change, it still hasn't stuck for Bettie, and "Dear Goldie" is how she starts the very next letter. "We could go places together and take trips on weekends to the mountains and the beach—also to Disneyland—and do a lot of things (and even go places to meet people) that we might not do if we were alone." None of these plans ever came to fruition.

THE 1980S

1981, January—Patton State Hospital, Patton, California

Roughly four months after Bettie's previous letter, she was arrested for accusa-tions of assaulting her elderly landlady—and her husband, when he came to his wife's rescue—with a knife. The current letter was sent during Bettie's first of two stints at Patton State psychiatric hospital for similar altercations; this time, she spent about twenty months there.

Her release date is six weeks away, and she says she may go to a board and care home for women in downtown Los Angeles when she leaves the hospital:

> *Maybe I can get a job nearby and walk to work. I would hate to have to ride those lousy buses twice a day; they're worse here than in Miami. The social worker on my unit said she will help me get located in a nice place where they will take care*

of my room and board until I get a job; then I won't have to borrow any money from anyone. I can stay at one of those homes up to four months. Many women who leave the state hospitals do that in order to get on their feet financially. It will be a big help to me.

But first things first: "I've been told the food is not so good in those places but I'm sure I can stand it for a few months. Besides, I can supplement the diet with fresh fruit and juices if I don't have much trouble finding work," she wrote. "Speaking of food—blast it!!! I've gained twelve pounds since Thanksgiving! I just couldn't resist the banana splits, three-fried-egg breakfasts, turkey and dressing, mincemeat pie, pumpkin cream pie, nuts, Christmas candy, and other goodies that I haven't had in ages." The food at Patton is pretty good, with Bettie's only complaint being the lack of fresh fruit and vegetables. "What they do with all those oranges out in the orchard I'll never know! We have oranges only once a week."

We get a glimpse into the emotional eating, yo-yo dieting, and weight struggles that hounded Bettie in her later years—and were central to her refusal to be seen in public when her fame resurged later:

When I first came here, I was depressed over the trouble I'd had with my lying, nervous-wreck landlady and landlord—so I ate everything put before me, including fattening desserts twice a day. In no time I gained 32 pounds. So many women have gotten fat in here that in April the dietician reinstituted the 1500-calorie diets for those who wanted to reduce. In five months I was back down to 134. I've also been doing calisthenics and aerobics fast-walking (to build up my heart, lungs and blood vessels) five days a week for over six months—since my arthritis quit hurting in my hips and right shoulder. . . . I'm in fairly good condition now and feel a thousand times better—look much better, too, of course. It's really a shame when we let ourselves go to pot physically—you know it hurts us emotionally as well. I like myself when I keep my weight down and the flab off.

Apparently, Goldie had mentioned in her last letter to Bettie that their mom and brother Jack forbade Goldie from going out during her recent visit to Nashville—accusing her of looking for a "sex orgy," and Goldie must have said something about their mother's jealous streak. To that, Bettie replied, "I quite agree that Mama is notorious for her jealousy—of <u>all</u> women, not just us. I wouldn't worry about it if I were you. It's just part of her makeup and she'll never change—just like Billy Neal."

She reminds Goldie that their mother usually gets over tiffs quickly— "except for that long-standing feud (or rather silence) between her and Lub for several years, over the coke bottle Mama claims Lub hit her over the temple with (which Lub denies doing; she says Mama was stoned and fell against the sharp edge of a desk in her house in Atlanta)."

She's working as a secretary for two of the fifteen psychologists at the hospital: "My employers look like Mutt and Jeff; one is less than five feet tall and the other is about six feet six. They're both very nice fellows." The gig pays only thirty cents an hour but it's "enough to keep me in coconut-pineapple juice (which I love) and peanuts at the canteen, plus shampoo, face cream, deodorant, and the like." The wife of one doc (the tall one) is a "rose grower par excellence," and he brings a new bunch for Bettie's desk each week.

She describes her setup at Patton, calling her particular unit the best in the hospital—reserved for patients with only minor emotional disturbances: "We're not locked up at Patton. It's such a huge place that it's like a small town. We can go anywhere on the grounds we like, except where the violent patients are," she notes without irony. "I haven't minded being here at all, except for the lack of privacy in the dormitory (there are 22 women in my dorm) and the snoring at night. Four or five of the women saw logs like lumberjacks."

For roughly a page and a half, she details at length all the amenities and activities available:

There's plenty to do; we have a large Olympic-size swimming pool, a baseball diamond, a football field, tennis courts, basketball courts, miniature golf, pool (billiards), ping-pong, all kinds of games, a nice well-equipped library, a big gym with weights and all kinds of exercise equipment, exercise classes, sewing and needlecraft classes, an O.T. shop (occupational therapy) with macramé, ceramics, painting, arts and crafts, etc. Each unit (or ward) has a large color TV, radios, and record players, a beauty shop, a piano, drums, and guitars, sewing room, laundry room with big washers and dryers and steam irons, and a huge recreation room with comfortable easy chairs and most of the latest books and magazines. I read a lot and sew while listening to television. We have the best of Hollywood's movies every Thursday in the dining room (last week we saw Robert Redford—my favorite leading man—in "Brubaker"; it was very good).

On top of all that, they periodically go on shopping trips, all-day picnics at the lake, to Anaheim Stadium to watch the Los Angeles Angels or Rams games, and more. They also have plenty of live entertainment in the hospital, including talent and variety shows, and weekly socials on the unit with dancing or bands playing.

Her unit had two holiday parties and received cosmetics as a gift from volunteer services. She also buys personal items with money that Harry and his wife June send to Bettie every couple of months.

She continues with some background info on the hospital, "There are a lot of show-business people—singers, dancers, musicians, and actors—at Patton. Most of them have had nervous breakdowns and committed a crime while under the influence of drugs" she explains. "Everybody who has committed a crime while having mental problems or who has been accused of a crime (like me) stays in here at least 18 months—that's the hospital policy. That's why I've been in this place so long. Once you're put in this hospital it takes a long time to get out, even if you're well."

Even in this setting, Bettie finds a love interest: "I have a 'boyfriend' that I see on the grounds (he's in another unit); he's a brain surgeon from India—quite good-looking. He's a very brilliant man, has written twelve books and pamphlets on the human brain, and has travelled all over the world—a most interesting man." He ended up at Patton because he was "emotionally overstrained" at a time when one of his patients died during surgery, she explains, and he was accused by the family of experimenting on the patient. "He denies it but admits he was overworked at the time; he's in here recuperating."

Some details of her case have been shared sparsely elsewhere, but here she gives a firsthand account of her side of the story, in which she denies ever even cutting the landlady or landlord:

I don't know how much you know of my case. I'll tell you briefly. I was having a hard time getting a permanent job (I was doing a few temporary stenographer stints) in L.A. and had had so much mental anguish with Jimmie for three months that I was depressed and down mentally. I had a bad nightmare and had very little sleep the night before my landlady and I got into it over the paring knife, so I wasn't feeling good at all. I was peeling a potato when I looked around and saw the nosey, hateful woman with her hands cupped over her face, peeking in my windows (as usual). It just flew all over me (I mean rage) and I went running to the door fussing at her and waving the knife in my hands—I completely forgot to put it down. When she saw me with the knife, she started hollering and jerked it out of my hand. My right thumb and middle finger were cut real bad. Her husband came running up and busted me over the head with a big hammer—he had been banging on something in his garage about twenty feet away. Some of the neighbors must have called the police; they came right away. The blood was pouring all over me from my head and hand. I saw all kinds of stars when he hit me with the hammer and almost passed out. I thought I was dying when I saw all the blood.

Bettie received seven stiches on her head, which was shaved all around the gash and made her look strange for weeks until her hair grew out. Her court date followed soon after:

Both of the creeps—I can't keep from calling them that—appeared in court with big casts on their arms up to the shoulders claiming I cut them all over their arms and hands. He said I cut the tendon in his right hand so badly that he couldn't do his work (he did odd jobs for people in the machine shop he had in the garage). The knife had already been knocked out of my hand by his wife and was on the ground when he came running out of the garage after she started yelling. He wasn't cut at all and neither was she; I'm the only one who got cut. He might have hurt his hand when he blasted my head so hard with that hammer. He was supposed to be 80 years old, but he looked and acted like a man forty years younger.

Bettie offers her thoughts on what led to the whole mess in the first place:

She didn't like me because he seemed to have a yen for me; he was always hanging around the cottage talking to me. When she'd see him near me, she would come banging out the back door making some feeble excuse to get him away from me. I'd hear her cursing him at the top of her voice; she had one of the dirtiest mouths I've ever heard in a woman. I could smell whiskey on her breath every time she came near me. They must have had some insurance policies and were trying to get money out of them when they lied about me cutting them. I don't know where they got those big casts—from some unscrupulous quack doctor I suppose.

Towards the end of the letter, it sounds like Goldie was having some difficulties of her own: "Sorry you are being so restricted by the doctors and social workers; they sound like a bunch of meddling busybodies with weird ideas," Bettie replied to what Goldie must have mentioned in her latest letter. "What difference does it make if you have a boyfriend or a lover? What business is it of theirs?"

1981, March—Fountain Guest Home, Santa Monica, California

Bettie has been released from Patton and is now at a transitional home in Santa Monica, in a lovely neighborhood only three blocks from the beach. She's living mostly with elderly retired folks, and she describes the people, the house and yard, and types of trees nearby: "tall Washingtonia palms on one side and giant date palms on the other side" of the street. "There is a unique birdbath in our yard and I can watch the birds cavorting from my windows; so far, all I've seen in it are two starlings. Over the patio is a pretty grape arbor with redwood latticework."

There's very little smog in the area, and every convenience is within walking distance. There's a new shopping mall only six blocks from her house; she doesn't mention it by name but is referring to Santa Monica Place, which was built in 1980 and is now home to the Bettie Page Store that opened in 2016. On a trip to the health food store on the first day of her arrival at the home, "I went hogwild and spent most of my money on dried banana chips (which I could gobble by the barrels full); yogurt; a delicious snack mix of peanuts, dried dates, chopped prunes, cashews, sunflower seeds, coconut, and pepitas (a long, greenish bean pod with a kernel in it); wheat germ cereal; and yogurt chips. They really tasted yummy since I haven't had anything like that in so long."

Contrary to what she had heard while still at Patton, the food at the home is satisfactory after all, as the main cook "believes in serving good healthy food—which pleases me to no end," but dinner is usually a soup and sandwich. "That's the only thing I don't like about the food—I wish we had more variety at suppertime."

Bettie is quite happy with her new digs overall and likes everything about being there except her grumbly elderly roommate, an eighty-four-year-old Ukrainian lady named Miriam Trotsky. "She had this cottage all by herself for several years and she still thinks she owns the bathroom. She's in there at least

(Well, Jack won't be getting any younger tomorrow.
Me? I wanta forget 'em!)

(64)

Dear Gloria,

Hi! Thought I'd let you know, I've moved out on my own again. I'm very happy about my new surroundings — just three blocks from the beach in a lovely neighborhood. My address is as follows:

Bettie Page
Fountain Guest Home (3A)
1018 Fourth Street
Santa Monica, California 90403

I live in a cottage with an 84-year-old Russian lady named Miriam Grotsky (an old maid); she was in love only once, when she was sixteen. She was born in the Ukraine and has some very interesting stories to tell about her childhood in Europe; she also lived in Germany before coming to America in 1929.

There are seventeen people here at Fountain (4 men and 13 women); most of them are retired and live at the home permanently. There are two rows of cottages joined together, each with its own porch and front yard. A main house with offices (the owners have a trucking business office here on the premises), a large living room, a recreation room, laundry room, and dining room and kitchen are in the back of the cottages. It's a very pretty place with lots of trees, shrubbery, and flowers. Fourth Street is lined with tall Washingtonia palms on one side and giant date palms on the other side. I've never seen such huge date palms; they must be a different variety from those short, widespread ones in south Florida. There are windows across one wall of my bedroom which looks out upon a thick row of the tallest banana trees (over)

twenty times a day—what she does in there is a mystery to me since I don't hear the toilet flushing often and she doesn't wear make-up." Among other complaints, "She is supposed to be hard of hearing—she wears a squeaky hearing aid—but if I even make a sound after 7 P.M. she hears it and starts grumbling."

Still, it's a whole lot better than living with twenty-one other women as she did at Patton: "I never had any privacy at the hospital. Somebody was always peeking over the commode room doors even when I was in the bathroom—and changing clothes was just like a floorshow, with so many gaping eyes all around watching."

As she wraps up the letter, she tells Goldie, "Take it easy—and get yourself a boyfriend no matter what they say. I wouldn't mind having one myself."

1981, December—Fountain Guest Home, Santa Monica, California

This seven-page typed letter is one of the overall pithiest letters in the bunch. Along the top, Bettie wrote:

> *Yes, Mama, I remember Orie Wilson telling me to look around while he snapped my picture when I'd just gotten out of bed, and hadn't even combed my hair. I could have clobbered him! I thought you would have burned that ugly snapshot. I'll keep it for posterity (Ha!) Wish I looked that good today!*

Ten months into her stay at the home, she now has a private room and bath all to herself. She also has a couple of friends: a ninety-five-year-old next-door neighbor named Mabel Knotts—"one of the sweetest ladies I've ever known, always cheerful and kind to everybody"—and a thirty-six-year-old Guatemalan woman named Marta "that I like very much," who lives behind her. Bettie often goes to Mabel's house to watch TV with her.

Before Bettie got the room to herself, she had—sure enough—"another trouble-causing nervous wreck for a roommate" for about a month, a sixty-seven-year-old Jewish woman who had been a botany and biology teacher at a Wisconsin college. (It seems safe to conclude that Bettie seemed to not get along well with roommates or landlords!) Here and there throughout this letter, she talks about "busybody" roommates and landladies—especially notable because this point in time is right between her two assault cases involving

(Yes, Mama, I remember Orie Wilson telling me to loop around while he snapped my picture when I'd just gotten out of bed, and hadn't even combed my hair. I could have clobbered him! I thought you would have burned that ugly snapshot. Thanks for sending it. I'll keep it for posterity!)

Saturday
Dec. 19th 81

6

Wish I looked that good today!

Dear Mama and Goldie,

Holidays full of happy days to both of you! I'm writing this letter (or should I say "book") to you jointly, with a copy to each of you, so I won't have to write it twice. I've just finished a long dissertation to Jack and to Harry and June (also a letter to Peggy), and I'm tired of writing. Also, I wrote in longhand most of this same information to Lub; it was 14 pages (or rather, 14 sides) and I was at it most of the afternoon. After I get this typed up and eat supper, I'm going next door to Mabel's and watch TV with her and Marta all evening. She's one of the sweetest ladies I've ever known, always cheerful and kind to everybody. Mabel was 95 last month; the owners of the Fountain properties gave a birthday party with a huge white cake for her (which we all enjoyed with butter pecan ice cream). I do a lot of shopping for her in the malls since she doesn't get around very well and is quite hard of hearing. She lets me use her refrigerator; all she keeps in it is catfood, juice, and milk. I'm doing my own cooking for breakfast and supper now; the only meal I eat in the dining room is lunch. Since I work upstairs, that makes it very convenient for me--also, lunch is the only good meal that is served at the Fountain Guest Home. I've been told the Retirement Home (which is also owned by Mr. Finch and his son) has much better food.

I bought, on sale at an appliance store, an electric broiler-oven with two burners which suits my purposes very well. I already had my blender (which I had shipped from Florida) and an electric frypan with calibrated heating from 250 degrees to 400 degrees. I used to cook things in it when I was paying for all three meals here several months ago, especially on days when the food was the worst.

I'm happy to have this nice room and bath all to myself now. For about a month in October, I had another trouble-causing nervous wreck for a roommate--a 67-yr.-old Jewish woman (with a Ph.D. degree who used to teach Botany and Biology in college in Wisconsin). She nearly drove me nuts grumbling and complaining about a different disease every day that she imagined she had--a real hypochondriac. She was paying on at least ten medical bills from as many doctors that she'd been to in the past year. Every one of them told her she had something wrong with her, but no two of these supposed ailments was the same. She would wake up in the morning while I was getting ready for work and grouch the whole time about how bad she felt, how poor she was, how cruel God was for taking her husband away from her (he died <u>eight years</u> ago), how unhappy her life had been, how nobody loved her, and on and on, especially repeating over and over that she was too sick to even get out of bed. Yet if she got a phone call from one of her friends, she'd practically jump out of the bed, be dressed in five minutes, and take off out the front door over to visit her. There was nothing the matter with her at all! She was talking herself into feeling bad by her constant grumping and griping about everything. I finally had to tell my boss that she was getting me depressed and I couldn't keep my mind on my work, so he made her move the next week. Of course, Mr. Finch is charging me extra for this private room and bath. Since it's the second largest room at the Fountain--or rather, cottages joined together in two rows--he said he couldn't let me have it for nothing. So I'm working <u>five</u> extra hours a week to pay for it. That's much too steep for what it's worth, since all I have for a kitchenette is a little alcove in a short hall or foyer between the bedroom and the bathroom, which has a cabinet with two drawers and two shelves below them. For cooking I use the top of the cabinet (for my stove), but the only sink I

landlords. This particular roommate was a hypochondriac, according to Bettie, and she complained incessantly about a long list of issues:

> *She would wake up in the morning while I was getting ready for work and grouch the whole time about how bad she felt, how poor she was, how cruel God was for taking her husband away from her (he died <u>eight years</u> ago), how unhappy her life had been, how nobody loved her, and on and on, especially repeating over and over that she was too sick to even get out of bed. Yet if she got a phone call from one of her friends, she'd practically jump out of the bed, be dressed in five minutes, and take off out the front door over to visit her. There was nothing the matter with her at all! She was talking herself into feeling bad by her constant grumping and griping about everything. I finally had to tell my boss that she was getting me depressed and I couldn't keep my mind on my work, so he made her move the next week.*

The landlord is charging her extra for the private space, though, and she's working five extra hours a week for him to pay for it.

She talks in detail about things she was learning about nutrition, positive thinking, and other healthy-living topics:

> *I'm eating only whole grain breads and cereals, liver, chicken, fish, ground round, eggs, cheese, milk, yogurt, sunflower seeds, blackstrap molasses, wheatgerm and bran, nutritional yeast, honey, kelp, fresh vegetables and fruits, also peanut butter and nuts. <u>I'm not eating any more junk food for the rest of my life in this body</u>; not only does it do nothing for you but put on the fat and flab, but they're discovering that the white flour, white sugar, white rice, white macaroni and spaghetti (and all of the foodstuff made out of them), together with*

all of the chemical additives in them, is causing cancer! So deliver me from all of the non-nutritive (and processed) "food"! I want to be as healthy as I can from here on out.

She was far ahead of her time in steering clear of processed foods, as experts were just beginning to discover and report on their negative health effects when consumed in excess.

"When I'm in shape, keep my body and mind exercised, eat only healthy foods, get enough sleep and rest, take sunbaths and airbaths, and live in peace with the people around me—like I am now—I'm an entirely different person than when I let myself go to pot all over," she reflects in one letter. ("Airbath" was her word for walking around in the nude, which she preferred to do outdoors.) She mentions going walking and jogging and doing calisthenics in Palisades Park in Santa Monica. "I've never been happier than walking along the beach flopping my bare feet in the water's edge."

Bettie even talks of plans to become an exercise instructor to the elderly: "I'm preparing for a whole new career and may even go back to school to take some courses in teaching physical fitness and healthy nutrition to seniors. I know a lot about both subjects, and could read up on it at the libraries and take notes (which I've already been doing), but in order to teach even garbage collecting nowadays, you've got to have some kind of certificate or degree."

She says, "I'm still doing my church work for the Lord," and describes going with a group from her church to different locations around Los Angeles to lead Bible study, help with church services, and "go witnessing."

She's taking various nutritional supplements and vitamins and feels far better with much more energy. "I feel a hundred times better and I haven't had a single cold," since she started taking them, she wrote, "even though the three feeble-minded men who eat lunch at my table have been coughing and sneezing in my face. . . . They're not really feeble-minded, it just seems that way because they never even say a word . . . unless I say something to them, it's just like being in the morgue around them."

As in the excerpt above, Bettie's letters are laced with wry humor despite her often-grim circumstances. In another part of the same letter, she mentions her fondness for Marta's canary, which Bettie enjoys tending to whenever Marta is out of town.

Recently she was gone for five weeks to her mother's outside of San Diego, and I kept the sweet little birdie near my bed close to the windows so he could look out at the banana trees, the hibiscus bush, and all of the geraniums in pots that I have in the windows. Also, from my room he could hear a lot of other birds outside in the trees; there are no trees on the other side where Marta lives.

The day before Bettie wrote this letter, Marta brought home a girlfriend for the canary, and they both laughed when he clumsily started mating with her not five minutes after being placed in the cage. "Like most other males today, that little character has no finesse, no tact, and no knowledge of how to please a female at all, and he ought to be clobbered!" she said.

Later she describes the mysterious fate of a gift basket of sweets and other treats that Mabel gave her (perhaps prompting that healthy eating vow she made earlier in the letter). She told Bettie to put it under the tree and save it for Christmas Day, and that was the plan:

And that's what I intended to do—honestly! I did put it under the tree; give me that much credit. But while I was writing to Lub (for the first time in two coon's ages), I looked over there and my mouth began to water. Well, it was a long letter! I just don't know where all the goodies went, but all of a sudden there was only an empty basket.

But still, she's not quite done indulging for the holiday season: "Now I may do that one more time this year (I'm told we will have nuts and candy on the dinner tables at the Fountain like we did at Thanksgiving—with another turkey dinner), but that's all!! If I keep it up I'll soon be as fat as Mrs. Fudge again—and the Lord deliver me from ever letting that happen again!!! I've had it with a capital H on being a fattie!"

Bettie describes the many reasons she loves living in Santa Monica and says she is looking for a job and apartment there. She says she may have to get a roommate, but she must have her own room: "I don't mind sharing the kitchen and bathroom with another person, as long as she's a positive-thinker and not a nettle-picker."

Quite hilariously, she goes on to lament all the griping and negativity she has observed in nine out of ten elderly people around her, and vows to never be like them. (This also adds more context to her well-known negative view of aging!)

> *After living around 'em for some time, and listening to all their operations, aches and pains, "hundred thousand" diseases, financial troubles, children-not-loving-them troubles, and ad infinitum (unendless), on a long list of things they gripe about all the time, <u>I've come to the conclusion that it's far better for my mental health to live around younger people</u>; they have a better attitude about almost everything, look forward to the future, still have their ideals and dreams, and have not become jaded and <u>down on the world and everybody in it</u> (like 9/10ths of the older men and women I've met lately). I realize there are a few elderly women like Mabel Knotts next door who don't <u>live in the unhappy past and grouch and groan about their ailments and what they haven't got</u> from morning to night—but it's been my experience so far that <u>these positive-thinking and enthusiastic-living seniors are very rare</u>, most unfortunately! <u>I'm training myself to be a Mable Knotts the rest of my life</u>; whenever she talks about her past life, most of what she tells is something pleasant. If she mentions a bad part of her life, she doesn't dwell on it for hours and keep yakking about it over and over again. . . . And Mabel is as poor as Job's turkey, living only on Social Security.*

Bettie was fifty-eight years old at the time of this letter and mentions that she's been dating a forty-two-year-old "Spanish fellow from Ecuador" she met on the beach while doing calisthenics. "We often stroll along there while he whistles pretty songs to me. Boy, can he whistle!" she wrote. When he asked her how old she was, she told him to guess, and he guessed late 30s. "I exclaimed, 'My, but you're a good guesser!' So that was that."

Between these frequent flashes of humor and the detailed descriptions of her doings and surroundings (remember when letter writers had to paint a mental picture?), the occasional wistful reflection or regret appears. In that same letter, for example, which was addressed to both Goldie and her mother, Bettie shares a short poem that Goldie wrote for her:

May the rains of life that fall upon
Your spirits now and then
Leave behind them a rainbow
To make life bright again.
And when the sun comes out,
As it surely will do,
May it bring a little joy
And happiness for you.

"I didn't have any idea that she is a poet as well as a painter. You missed your calling, Goldie (like I did)." Bettie was referring to her dashed dream of becoming a Hollywood actress.

Again, ironically, she describes celebrity sightings and says there are quite a few living in Santa Monica. In a poignant line reflecting the fact that Bettie is a star but still an outsider, she says, "I often see TV stars and other famous faces in the glassed-in dining room at Michaels" as she passes by.

There had been a "History of Cheesecake" pageant held at the new shopping mall a few weeks earlier, and Phyllis Diller was the star. Bettie had signed up to volunteer as a 1950s pinup model but changed her mind "when I began to realize that some of the old fogeys who live at the Fountain would see the pageant and find out that I had once been a pinup model; about four of the old biddies here are so old-fashioned in their thinking that they would create a stink and cause me to have to move (which I don't want to do at this time)."

A few months earlier, she had experienced "the most romantic moment I've had in many years" when she attended a concert by the US Air Force Band in Lincoln Park:

I was sitting in the front row on the grass and had been thinking how good-looking the Japanese-American male vocalist was (around 40ish), when he began to sing my modern-day favorite love song,

"Lady." He came right over to me and sang the whole thing directly to me, about half of it <u>kneeling at my feet</u> and holding my hand, all the time looking deep into my eyes. Naturally, I was flabbergasted and most pleased and excited. On the beginning of the last stanza, I squeezed his hand and he squeezed mine back and smiled. Only he and I knew it. I know we were both thinking of the words of the song and wishing we had found such a love in our lives. (Harry and I had a taste of it in the beginning of our relationship, but my troubles with his ex-wife and their three children ruined everything between us). . . . That sweet experience makes me feel good every time I think of it. Lovely moments like that don't come along very often when the years begin to pile up on you—or need I remind either of you of that tragic aspect of aging?

She hasn't given up on love: "It still happens to older people occasionally—not the great passionate flame of youth but a more gentle, companionable love. . . . One main reason I'm keeping in shape these days is just in case I meet someone who really turns me on—I don't care if he's 30 or 70, as long as we are compatible and enjoy being together."

It is striking how poor she was as other people made money off her image. She apologized to her mom that she wouldn't receive the ten dollars Bettie had intended to send her until after Christmas because she was so broke: She said the roughly twenty dollars she spent on a Christmas tree, lights for it, and a gift for her housemate—that optimistic Mable Knotts—"busted me" financially. Though she mentions repeatedly over the decades how broke and bad off she was, that hope, sweetness, and sharpness remained.

This letter gives the feeling that things are finally working out for Bettie, that she's on the cusp of embarking on a whole new, positive path in life—the proverbial second chance, even. It's clear that her spirits have been lifted and she's feeling more content and optimistic than she has sounded in any of the previous letters.

Sadly, before she was able to turn a new leaf in her career or love life, she was in court again for another altercation with a landlord just six months later. This time she was found not guilty by reason of insanity and sentenced to ten years at Patton State.

1983, March—Patton State Hospital, Patton, California

Back in unit 35 at Patton State Hospital, Bettie writes, "Dear Mama, I hope you're well enough now to throw your walker to the winds (on second thought maybe you'd better keep it just in case)."

She mentions that Goldie had recently told her that she'd lost weight but then gained back sixteen pounds in about three months. (Here and elsewhere in her letters, it is evident that she and Goldie shared their dieting and body image troubles—not surprising given the stranglehold that diet culture had on women back then; although dieting and eating disorders are certainly rampant today, awareness has increased regarding the dangers of dieting, and the growing body positivity movement offers more balanced perspectives.)

Bettie can relate to Goldie's latest weight battle, even without the treats she enjoyed on her previous unit, where they had a cooking class. She misses all the "yummy 'fattening' things like chocolate fudge with walnuts, German chocolate cake, doughnuts (which didn't come out right), pizza, French fried onions, brownies, etc."

Even so, she's been gaining several pounds per month herself:

> Sad to say I've been gaining an average of about four pounds each month since the first of the year because I've been so down and disgusted at the latest antics my ex-landlady has been up to. (I've just been eating everything in sight around here, including the fattening desserts and night-time snacks. That's why I haven't written but one letter in three months; I just haven't felt like doing any writing.)

This time Bettie is accused of attacking her elderly landlady, Leonie Haddad, with a knife and stabbing her numerous times. She explains that Ms. Haddad

Dec. 18, 1989

Dear Gloria,

Hi! I hope you are feeling well and chipper these days. I'm doing as well as could be expected under the circumstances. Please forgive me for not writing to you! I don't write to anybody very often because of this terrible arthitis in my fingers.

I'm expecting to leave this hospital any day now. I have to go to a rehabilitation center for about a year before I am completely released.

Jimmie came to see me a few months ago. He is looking well and strong. He's still in Las Vegas at 117 N. 9th Street, zip code 89101 in case you don't have his address. I sleep in a room with two other women. They are good roommates. We have a new stationary bicycle on our unit. I ride it for thirty minutes every day. I also do calisthenics for forty-five minutes every other day. I feel much better when I exercise. I'm on a diet again. I need to lose about twenty-five pounds. It's so easy to put on weight in here because we sit down so much watching TV.

I was on television for about ten minutes on the Entertainment Tonight show on Nov. 7th. It was all pin-ups of the 1950's. Jack saw the show; he wrote me about it.

I do a lot of reading. We have a very good library. It's not doing my eyes any good.

Write to me if you feel like it. I'll let you know my new address. Take care, Sincerely, Bettie

is suing the State of California and Patton State for releasing her too soon when she was there the first time.

Bettie doesn't offer her account of the current situation, leaving it at this: "It's a long ugly story full of one lie after another, and I won't bore you with the details of it; besides, it puts me in a lousy mood and makes me feel bad just to think about it. The less said the better, I think." What's more, "She's the biggest liar and the most money-mad female I ever had the misfortune to room with in my life. I don't know how I could be so unlucky to meet her," Bettie exclaims, clearly in denial about her mental illness and completely lacking insight into what led her back to Patton.

In a 1998 interview with *Playboy*, she claimed that she didn't cut the woman, only threatened her because she wouldn't give her rent receipts that she needed in order to keep her social security benefits. She told the magazine, "I wasn't that sick. I might have cut her if she hadn't given me the rent receipts, but I would not have killed her. I never had that feeling even when I was mentally sick, but now it's on my record: assault with a deadly weapon with intent to commit murder."

She was surprised to hear in her mother's previous letter that Harry and June had divorced, and was sorry to hear it.

"I sure would like to see all of you . . . but I will probably be kept in this hospital a long time," she predicts. "There's nothing I can do about that, so I'm trying to resign myself to it and take things one day at a time."

1989, December—Patton State Hospital, Patton, California

Now in a different unit at the hospital, Bettie tells Goldie she doesn't write very often because of "this terrible arthritis in my fingers."

She was expecting to leave Patton any day to go to a rehab center, where she was to stay for about a year before being fully released. She sleeps in a room with two other women—who she says are good roommates for a change.

She rides a stationary bike for thirty minutes a day and does calisthenics— that longtime mainstay of her fitness regimen—for forty-five minutes every other day. "I feel much better when I exercise," she says, adding that she's on a diet again and needs to lose about twenty-five pounds. She's also doing a lot of reading.

Here we start to see her fame resurgence and how she learned about it: "I was on television for about ten minutes on the *Entertainment Tonight* show on November 7th. It was all pin-ups of the 1950s." Their brother Jack had seen it and wrote to tell Bettie about it.

THE 1990S

1990, December—Foothill Health & Rehab, Sylmar, California

For the second letter in a row, Bettie greets her sister with "Dear Gloria," and asked how she's feeling these days, as she hasn't heard from Goldie in a long time. Bettie had been out of Patton for four and a half months and says she will be at this rehab center for at least a year. "I'm reading a lot. My therapist

brought me a large box full of Harlequin romances, outer space adventures, and westerns. . . . I've just finished reading Charles Dickens' David Copperfield. I am beginning to read the Bible through again," she reports. "I'm doing calisthenics for one hour every other day. I walk the halls for half an hour every day when I don't go outside."

She explains that she had worried that she had cancer due to some intestinal issues she'd been having, but she went to the doc and was relieved to find out it was nothing serious. Finally, "It will be a very happy Christmas for me this year, thank the Lord."

1991, December—Pacoima, California

After apologizing for not writing for a long time, Bettie tells Goldie, "I still think of you often and hope you're not mad at me."

Bettie has been living with ten men and women at a board and care home called Hillview (which still operates today) since August. Again, food and weight get a spotlight: "We have a very good cook named Pete. I've already gained ten pounds in four months. We had a sumptuous Thanksgiving dinner. I ate three small pieces of three different pies: pumpkin, apple, and pecan. Delicious!" The aging woes get another mention too: "I've decided I hate old age. I

have so many ailments that I never had when I was young," which she goes on to itemize.

She likes to read *Reader's Digest* magazines that her brother Jack sends her (she hasn't heard from Jimmie, who's been living in Las Vegas for some time, in a couple of years), and she watches movies on TV every night. Also, "I have discovered the *Smithsonian* magazine lately. It has a whole rafter of good articles and pictures something like the *National Geographic*, which I like very much."

She went to the movies and saw Bruce Willis in *The Last Boy Scout* and "It had undoubtedly the filthiest language of any movie I have ever seen. . . . Motion pictures are just not what they used to be." She saw *Gone with the Wind* on TV recently "for the umpteenth time" and never gets tired of watching it.

Bettie is still riding a stationary bike thirty minutes daily and walking for forty minutes per day; she can't do calisthenics because she hurt her arm.

Her ex-husband Harry still sends her money, and she's trying to find a part-time job with no luck. She was told she's too old for secretarial work, and the arthritis in her hands makes it difficult to type. "Just living on social security doesn't give me much spending money," she said. "I'd like to be a companion for some nice lady, but I don't have any experience or references, unfortunately."

December 1993—Arleta, California

The note written inside this Christmas card to Goldie is relatively brief:

> *Dear Gloria,*
>
> *Hi! I hope you are well and kicking. I'm doing as well as could be expected with arthritis all over my body now. I have been having a terrible time with it for the past couple of months. Every day I hate old age more and more.*
> *Tell Ronnie hello for me when you see him. Take care of yourself and let me hear from you once in a while.*
>
> *Love, Bettie*

Earlier that year, Bettie had been featured on *Entertainment Tonight*, and Jack had written to Goldie to tell her about the show. In that letter from Ron's archives, Jack said he and Bettie had both been interviewed for the segment

Dec. 17th

Dear Gloria,

Hi! I hope you are well and kicking. I'm doing as well as could be expected with arthitis all over my body now. I have been having a terrible time with it for the past couple of months. Every day I hate old age more and more.

Tell Ronnie hello for me when you see him. Take care of yourself and let me hear from you once in a while.

May your joys
be many at Christmas...
and may the year ahead
bring all life's
best gifts to you

Love,
Bettie

DEC 93

(though Bettie's part was only audio, of course), and each of them were paid five hundred dollars. Jack gave Bettie his portion, and he helped her out in lots of other ways over the years. In one of her letters, Bettie told Goldie Jack was the "best brother any sister could ever have."

Quite amusingly, in Goldie's return letter to Jack, she seems to be assuring him that their sister never posed nude:

There wasn't any porno back then—none that I saw. Nudity wasn't allowed in the magazines— except the one for the nudist colony. I kept a lot of her pictures in a few old magazines I bought back in the '50s. She wore costumes or a bikini. I used to look at the magazines in the book stands to see if there was a picture of her in them and if I had a little change I would buy it. I didn't buy many—I was too poor and broke all the time. The photos I saw of her looked okay to me.

December 1995—Granada Hills, California

"Dear Gloria,

"Hi! Long time no hear. I wish you all the happiness in the world at this Christmastime and forever." She apologizes again for not writing sooner: "This lousy arthritis in my hands makes it so hard for me to write that I just haven't been doing it. . . . Sorry to say but I'm not feeling very good these days." She describes several ailments, including a chronic, terrible bladder infection.

Bettie is now living in an adult residential care home, and she gets along well with the two guys she shares a house with. "For the first time in seventeen years I cooked a big roast hen and giblet dressing with all the trimmings for Thanksgiving. I invited my best friend, the artist Dave Stevens. He takes me out to dinner and to the movies and concerts frequently." (Stevens is the illustrator of *The Rocketeer* comics, which includes a character based on Bettie and later became a Disney movie. He is credited as a major reason for her resurgence in fame.)

She mentions her biography by Karen Essex and James Swanson, which will soon be published: "A book about my life is coming out in January. I'm hoping to make some money from it—that is, if it sells.

"I've become an A1 cable TV addict. Almost every night I plop down on the couch with my feet propped up on pillows on the coffee table and watch the good old movies and movie stars till the wee hours of the morning." She also spends a lot of time pruning and watering the plants on the patio and in the yard. "I like this house and neighborhood better than any place I've ever lived," she says.

1996, April—Granada Hills, California

Goldie had promised to send a letter last Christmas—"I'm still waiting for it (ha!)," Bettie wrote.

4/15/96

Dear Gloria,

    Hi! Long time, no hear! You promised to write me a letter last Christmas; I'm still waiting for it (ha!). Hope you are well.

    Jack tells me that you like your new apartment and neighborhood much better than your old address. I'm very glad to hear it. From what you wrote me, you were long overdue for a change in your surroundings. Me? I'm very happy to be living in beautiful Granada Hills; in fact, I like the house, the walled-in patio, and the front yard (with all of the lovely plants and trees) better than any place I've ever lived. I

"I'm very happy to be living in beautiful Granada Hills; in fact, I like the house, the walled-in patio, and the front yard (with all of the lovely plants and trees) better than any place I've ever lived." She again mentions that she shares the house with two men and they "get along fine—just like brothers and sister.

"My health has gone to pot in the last couple of years," with widespread arthritis, bladder problems, bronchitis, and pneumonia. "I felt so bad I was sure I was going to kick the bucket," then, following more details: "Well, I guess you're tired of hearing about my ailments."

Bettie has enclosed a copy of her biography, which had been published the previous month. "Try not to be shocked when you see the three or four full frontal nudes in there," she warns. "The editors promised Dave Stevens, the artist and my best friend, that none of those pictures would be in the book, but then the dirty louses went ahead and told the art director to put 'em in there anyway. Except for that, I am very pleased with the book."

Inside Goldie's copy, Bettie wrote:

To Gloria,

You will always be Goldie to me. The best of everything to you always.

Love,
Bettie

1996, December—Granada Hills, California

"Dear Gloria, I hope you are well and chugging along. I am okay except for the lousy arthritis and bladder trouble," Bettie reports. She had an operation for the bladder problem, but it didn't help at all. "I wish I had never heard of that urologist."

She had also had another terrible cancer scare; the doc thought a spot detected on a mammogram might be breast cancer, but when the biopsies revealed it was not, "I was so relieved that I burst into tears."

1997, December—Granada Hills, California

With her renewed fame now in full swing, Bettie sent this six-page photocopied
letter to her fans, and she wrote a letter to Goldie along the left side of the pages
that continued onto an extra sheet of paper.

Dear Goldie,
Long time no hear! I'm
glad to have your nice card
+ letter of Dec. 20th and to know
you are chugging along and
hanging in there, despite your
obnoxious problems with
landlords and neighbors.
It's too bad you have to put
up with such
creeps.

Believe me,
everything in
my lifestory
book really
happened to me,
good and bad.

I take Calcium,
magnesium,
B-complex (with
extra Pantothenic
acid for my
lousy arthritis),
Vitamins A, C,
D, E, and K, plus
several herbs,
bee pollen, lecithin,
kelp, evening
primrose oil, fatty
acids, all of the
minerals, etc.
I haven't had a
cold in three
years and have
almost as much
energy as I did
when I was young.
I also eat a lot
of fruits and
vegetables. My
goal is to live
to be a hundred.

This form letter (which
I sent to everybody
mostly fans— will
explain why you didn't
get a Christmas card
from me.

①

Friday
Dec. 19, 1997

Please forgive me for
not writing to you sooner. I
know some of you have come
to the conclusion that I'm just
an ingrate and you will never
hear from me.   that's understandable.

I am sorry to have to tell
you that 1997 has _not_ been my
year. I have been plagued with
two terrible cancer scares beginning
about the time of my birthday. My
yearly mammogram revealed that
I had a cyst and several calcium
deposits in my left breast. the
radiologist was convinced it was
cancer, and so was I. I was worried
sick because two of my aunts died
of breast cancer and my grand-
mother died of stomach cancer.
I had to have two different kinds
of biopsies before the surgeon

In the fan letter she starts: "Please forgive me for not writing sooner. I know some of you have come to the conclusion that I'm just an ingrate and you will never hear from me. That's understandable. I'm sorry to tell you that 1997 has not been my year." She goes on to describe some of her health problems and two cancer scares—one involving the possibility of bone cancer for which she had to undergo magnetic resonance imaging (MRI) testing:

I had never heard of an MRI, and I never want to hear of one ever again! They made me lie on my back on a very narrow board with rollers and shoved me into a huge contraption that looked like a concrete mixer; the hole in it was just barely large enough for me to squeeze into with my arms crossed over my chest. I was not allowed to move at all for over an hour and a half! It was stifling hot under there and I could hardly breathe! Finally, I had to yell out, "I want to get out of here!" I felt like I was going to die in that thing; it's some sort of electromagnet.

Like the breast cancer scare, this one also turned out to be a nonissue. "I believe—and so do the doctors—that all of the umpteen supplements I've been taking twice a day with meals has built up my immune system so much that my body's army of t-cells and other 'warriors' are able to fight off and destroy the free radicals that cause cancer."

She was unable to write the fan letter herself because a cabdriver had slammed her right hand in the car door, so one of her roommates wrote it for her. "I've been asking the Lord why all this has happened to me one on top of the other. I keep asking myself, 'What have I done to deserve it?'"

The letter closes with: "Thank you for all your kindness, thoughtfulness, and generosity; I really appreciate it even though it might not have appeared so."

—

In the letter to Goldie along the sides of the fan letter, Bettie wrote, "I'm glad to have your nice card & letter of Dec. 20th and to know you are chugging along and hanging in there despite your obnoxious problems with landlords and neighbors. It's too bad you have to put up with such creeps." It's interesting to hear that, like Bettie, Goldie had issues with landlords and others living nearby, whether real or imagined.

Bettie then changes the subject, saying, "Believe me, everything in my life story book really happened to me good and bad."

Bettie describes the slew of vitamins and supplements she's taking, and despite the other health complaints, she hasn't had a cold in three years and has "almost as much energy as I did when I was younger," she claims. "I also eat a lot of fresh fruits and vegetables. My goal is to live to be a hundred and be in as good health as possible. If I have to be bed-ridden or in a wheelchair I would rather end it all." She bought a lot of books on antiaging and longevity and lists numerous things she is doing to eat healthfully.

She is still living in the house where Pete cooks, which she moved to three and a half years ago, but now she makes her own food. Since giving up his grub, she has lost twenty-six pounds but says still needs to lose about twenty more: "I'm having a terrible time getting the flab off. Eating is my greatest pleasure in old age; I just refuse to starve myself. But I've just got to get back down to 135 or 40, or I'll never make it to a hundred."

She speaks, as she does several times throughout the years, of her brother Jimmie's gambling addiction, and mentions the only two times she's tried gambling in her life (including betting fifty cents at a dog race when she lived in Miami). "I've always been afraid I'd become addicted to gambling like so many people do (including Jimmie). That's why I drank only a few glasses of wine in all of my seventy-four years—fear of becoming an alcoholic."

1999, January—Granada Hills, California
(Late card intended for Christmas 1998)
At nearly seventy-six years old, Bettie writes:

> *I hope you are as well and in as good health as possible, in view of all the ailments and other degenerative conditions that we are plagued with due to O.A. Do you know what that stands for? Make a wild guess. I never say the words, only the initials, when I'm thinking about it. That way it seems to hold back the years and I feel younger. I've got a*

big sign up on my bedroom wall, among others, that I'm trying with all my might to do: <u>I must practice positive thinking at all times and eliminate negative thinking.</u>

(That was her underlining, as it is in the excerpt below.)
She continues:

Do you know it makes all the difference in the world as to how you feel if you don't moan and groan about all the bad things that have happened to you throughout your past life, if you put it all behind you and <u>expect good things to come to you. Chances are they will just because you believe it.</u> As part of my studies on anti-aging and longevity (I'm trying to live to be 100+ in good health as much as possible), I've been reading a lot about <u>the power of the mind to heal.</u> You know there are two truisms: <u>you are what you eat and you are what you think! Your mind influences every part of your body. You are only as old as you think. Your mind affects your body's ability to make itself sick or well. Your thoughts determine whether you become old as you age or stay young.</u> How you think results in how you feel. Unhappy emotions and poor self-image can lead to disease. <u>I know from personal experience that this works,</u> Goldie (oops, I mean Gloria). Maybe you should copy all of this in big letters and put it up on the wall where you can read it every day—like I do—and <u>DO it!!!</u> Believe me, that's the best possible New Year's resolution you could make.

Then she proceeds to apologize that the card won't make it in time for the holidays; Bettie could only just walk again after a painful bout of plantar fasciitis—"just another symptom of o.a., the doctor says"—kept her from making the trip to the post office.

the words, ② only the initials,
when I'm thinking about it.
That way it seems to hold
back the years and I feel
younger. I've got a big sign up
on my bedroom wall, among
others, that I'm trying with
all my might to do:
<u>I must practice positive
thinking at all times and
eliminate all negative thinking.</u>

   Do you know it makes all
the difference in the world as
to how you feel if you don't
moan and groan about all the
bad things that have happened
to you throughout your past
life, if you put it all behind
you, and <u>expect good things to
come to you. Chances are they
will just because you believe
it.</u> As a part of my studies on
anti-aging and longevity (I'm ↓

JAN 9-99

Dear Gloria —

<u>Wishing you</u>

the brightest of holidays

and the happiest of years.

   Most sincerely,
     Bettie
Greetings! Long time, no hear!
I hope you are as well and in
as good health as possible, in
view of all the ailments
and other degenerative conditions
that we are plagued with
due to O.A. Do you know
what that stands for? Make
a wild guess. I never say →

③ trying to live to be 100+ in
good health as much as possible).
I've been reading a lot about
<u>the power of the mind to
heal.</u> You know, there are two
truisms: <u>you are what you
eat and you are what you
think!</u> Your mind influences
every part of your body. You
are only as old as you think.
Your <u>mind affects your body's
ability to make itself sick or
well.</u> Your thoughts determine
<u>whether you become old as you
age, or stay young.</u> How you
think results in how you feel.
Unhappy emotions and poor
self-image can lead to disease.
<u>I know from personal experience
that this works.</u> Goldie (oops,
I mean Gloria). Maybe you
should copy some of this in big
letters and put it up on the
wall where you can read it

JAN 9-99

Bettie still talks to Lub on the phone now and then, although she hasn't seen her in years, and Lub's daughter Tammy is a huge fan of her aunt and has been collecting Bettie memorabilia for years.

Her brother Jack visits Bettie often, and during his latest visit, they took a road trip together:

> *We went to Las Vegas to see Jimmie and all of the wonderful sights that have sprung up in what used to be a small town with one mile-and-a-half street downtown called The Strip. Now it is a five-mile-long wide boulevard with another one paralleling it, both loaded with the most beautiful, myriad-lighted hotels and casinos you could ever imagine. Jimmie says there are over a million people living in Las Vegas now.*

Perhaps surprisingly given their earlier tiffs, Jimmie has suggested that Bettie move to Vegas, but "I am very happy where I'm living now and have no intentions of moving until the Lord takes me out of this body," she wrote.

"I pray the good Lord God will bless you and me with the best years of our lives throughout 1999. With God all things are possible, you know."

1999, December—Granada Hills, California

> *Greetings! Hope you and Ronnie are well and kicking. I'm doing okay except for my lousy arthritis and a painful heel spur that's been plaguing me for five months. Buy yourself a little something with the enclosed 50 bucks. I won't write much because I have umpteen fan letters to answer before Christmas. God bless you. Love, Bettie*

Enclosed –
A POSTAL MONEY ORDER
FOR 50.

Dear Gloria,

Wishing you a bright,

old-fashioned kind of Christmas

and much happiness throughout the year.

Greetings! Hope you and Ronnie are well and kicking. I'm doing okay except for my lousy arthritis and a painful heel spur that's been plaguing me for five months. Buy yourself a little something with the enclosed 50 bucks. I won't write much because I have umpteen fan letters to answer before christmas. God bless you.
Love,
Bettie DEC 99

THE 2000S

2000, November—Granada Hills, California

In this last note to her dear sister, written inside a birthday card, she's back to calling her Goldie. "You promised to answer my last letter but I've never received a word," she starts.

"I'm doing as well as could be expected with umpteen ailments. . . . Despite all of the ravages of aging, I'm still counting my blessings and thanking the good Lord that I'm as well and healthy as I am."

She apologizes for forgetting to send an autographed photo to Ron as requested and says, "The worst of all of my degenerative setbacks is loss of memory. I have to write everything down on paper or I won't remember to tweet -> (you figure that out.)"

2000, December–Granada Hills, California

This is the last note of the bunch (see image below), written inside a Christmas card to Ron and his then-wife. After apologizing for the late mailing, Bettie writes:

> *Ronnie, I just wrote your mother that I can't remember if I did or did not send you a thank-you card for being "my biggest fan" (as she put it). In any case, I am thanking you now. It's very sweet of you. Take care.*

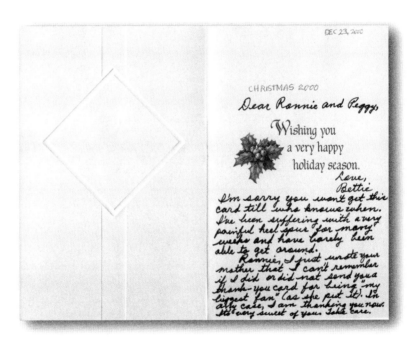

Goldie in 1951.

PART IV
Meet Goldie Jane

Had it not been for Goldie's careful efforts to preserve these treasures and pass them down to Ron, this book simply could not have happened. She and Bettie kept in touch as best they could as they got into their later years, which wasn't easy because of their various health issues.

Ron recalls the final communication between his mom and aunt: When Goldie was diagnosed with late-stage cervical cancer not long before her death from the disease in 2004, Ron dialed Bettie so the two could have one last conversation. They apologized to each other for not keeping in closer touch, chatted a bit, and then Ron clearly remembers Goldie saying to Bettie, "Well, I'm on my way out."

Thanks to her foresight, Bettie's fans can get to know the pinup queen on a whole new level. Goldie had hoped to have a modeling career, too, but it didn't pan out that way. While Bettie turned out to be the star of the family, Goldie was a fascinating woman herself who shared a lot in common with her legendary sister but had her own unique talents too. She also steadily encouraged Ron to develop his and to pursue his dream of being a musician. Here, he shares some details of his mother's life.

Goldie at age sixteen in 1942. The photo was hand-colored by Goldie.

Goldie Jane Page was born on November 7, 1925, in Rome, Georgia. Times were very hard for the Page family in those days; I remember Mom telling me about how poor they were, and how my grandpa had stolen a car, got caught, and was sent to jail for a bit.

Even though they were barely getting by, Goldie enjoyed drawing pictures from an early age, the beginning of what would turn out to be a life-long love of art. She also had a passion for music, poetry, and telling a good joke. I remember that when Bettie, Mom, and my grandma Edna would get together, one of the first things they would do was tell each other the latest jokes they had heard— and I remember some of the ones my grandma told were pretty risqué!

While I was growing up in southern Illinois, just across the Mississippi River from St. Louis, Missouri, Mom was always busy. She loved gardening and grew many flowers along our driveway and in her beautiful round garden that she made in our backyard. She also sewed some of her own dresses and other clothing, and she told me how she would sew her own bikinis and dancing costumes too.

Aside from doing a few modeling shoots with her sister Bettie, she was also a burlesque dancer in nightclubs before meeting my dad, Mel Brem. I remember her telling me that Bettie would get a bit jealous if the photographer would pay a little too much attention to my mom on the photo shoots; there was always a friendly rivalry between the two of them in those days.

My parents dated for about two years and got married on July 14th, 1956, at the Davidson County Courthouse in Nashville, Tennessee. Goldie then retired from dancing to focus on starting a family. A couple of years later, they had their only child—me!

Looking back, I truly had a happy childhood, thanks to both of my parents. At a time when the "do it yourself" spirit was very much alive, my mom taught me how to use her sewing machine while my dad taught me about working on cars, woodworking, and other mechanical things. Mom was also a great cook,

Wedding photo, 1956.

and I really learned a lot from her. She would often set a very nice table for diner, sometimes complete with candlelight! She was highly creative and a great artist, and she could even do a bit of woodworking herself. When I was a young child, she helped build me a playhouse and a toy grandfather clock.

Mom had a great love of photography, and it seemed she was always taking pictures. She often had me taking pictures also; I remember helping with the flashbulbs and the film from an early age. I think the two of us took more photographs than anyone I knew of growing up. I remember always having a camera in my hand. She would sometimes take her own modeling pictures; she had devised a way of tripping the shutter on the camera with a small string while she would pose for the photos.

Mom took up oil painting in the early 1960s and quickly became quite good at it. She joined a couple of different artist guilds, and for years, she often won first or second place at the local county fair. I remember how proud we were when there was a big article about her in the local newspaper on her winnings at the St. Clair County Fair. She went on to display her oil paintings for many years throughout the St. Louis metropolitan area at various art shows, galleries, and shopping malls.

My dad and I would help out with the art shows too. We would build the picture frames and the canvas stretcher frames for the paintings, and Dad even built a large display stand and a nice oak easel for her to paint with. Mom later ended up teaching oil painting classes and had her own small art gallery in south St. Louis later in life. She always had a fondness for landscapes and florals in particular.

Mom was always taking me places when I was a kid. In the summertime, we would often go see the world-class performances at the St. Louis Municipal Opera in Forest Park. I remember seeing great plays like *Oklahoma*, *South Pacific*, *The Wizard of Oz*, and *Phantom of the Opera*—I even saw the Andrews Sisters sing and met the comedian Red Skelton! She also really enjoyed visiting the St. Louis Art Museum and studying the works of the great masters; Vincent Van Gogh was one of her favorites.

We enjoyed the Forest Park Zoo and the McDonnell Planetarium, and we would go check out the great displays in the department store windows at Christmastime in downtown St. Louis. Some of my favorite memories are the trips up and down the Mississippi River on the great steam-powered SS *Admiral* riverboat, and hearing its steam calliope play a song!

My mom was always supportive of me when I wanted to learn to play music at an early age. She went to bat for me when my dad didn't think it was too good an idea. When I was five, my Mom would take me on the bus over the river to downtown St. Louis to take piano lessons. Later, on my own, I took up playing drums at age seven and then the guitar a couple years later.

MY OLD MAGAZINES

				PRICE
1	FLIRT	DEC	1953	.25
2	TITTER	DEC	1953	.25
3	GALA	JAN	1954	.25
4	FLIRT	FEB	1954	.25
5	TITTER	JUNE	1954	.25
6	GLAMOUR	DEC	1954	.25
7	MAN'S MAGAZINE	DEC	1954	.25
8	EYEFUL	DEC	1954	.25
9	BEAUTY PARADE	MARCH	1955	.25
10	PEEP SHOW	SPRING	1955	.25
11	FROLIC	APRIL	1955	.25
12	GALA	MARCH	1957	.25
13	GLAMOUR PARADE	DEC	1957	.35

SMALL ONES

CARNIVAL	DEC	1953	6X8 .25
SHOW	SEPT	1954	.10
SHOW	DEC	1954	.10
PHOTO	JAN	1955	.25
STARE	APRIL	1955	6X8 .25
EYE	APRIL	1955	6X8 .25
VUE	APRIL	1956	.25
BOLD	JAN	1957	4X6 .15

Goldie's collection of magazines that featured Bettie.

Bettie would often ask how I was doing playing music, as she was interested in playing the guitar too. Even though Mom didn't play any instruments, she did take up writing song lyrics and ended up writing a couple of small books full of lyrics. She always wanted me to help write music to go with her lyrics and to record some of them too. Thanks to my mom's great help, I'm still playing and writing music to this day.

When I was a child, I was told that my aunt Bettie and my mom were both models in the 1950s. But it wasn't until I was nineteen years old, when Mom went up into our attic and brought down a box full of 1950s magazines she had collected over the years, that I fully understood just what kind of modeling they had done. I had no idea how extensive my aunt's modeling career had been. To say the least, it was really an eye-opening experience!

My mom never did feel that the name Goldie was very fitting for her, as she had naturally long black hair just like her sister Bettie, so she went as far as to have her first name legally changed to Gloria in the 1950s, but to Bettie and the rest of the Page family she remained Goldie!

Christmas Day, 1951 Photoshoot

New York Photos, 1951

Miscellaneous Modeling Photos, 1950s

Epilogue

From the time of Bettie's final letter until her death in 2008, her fame continued to skyrocket as her health declined, though she appeared to be in good condition for her age when she was photographed a couple of different times at the Playboy Mansion in the early 2000s.

She has conveyed in interviews that she was content being a homebody, staying up late nursing that cable TV "addiction," and when she was well enough, she would dance around the house as part of an aerobics routine she created for herself. Bettie allowed a few close friends into her private world who kept her company and took her on outings periodically.

Well before her death in 2008, she had become fully aware of just how admired and loved she was, and she enjoyed interacting with her adoring devotees. In a chatroom-style interview with fans, these were her parting words: "I thank you for your love and concern. It makes me feel good knowing you're out there. Kisses to all of you too and hugs too."

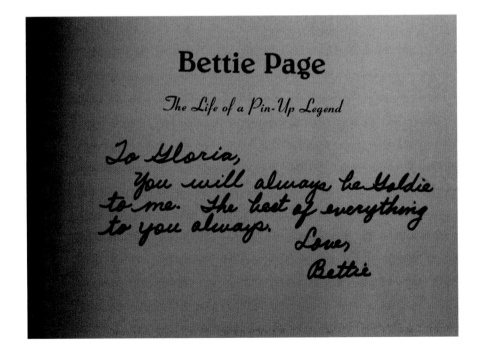

Acknowledgments

Tori: My deepest gratitude to all who have allowed me the incredible honor of getting to know Bettie and telling her story: Ron Brem, Goldie Jane, El Uno, Mark Mori, and Coleen O'Shea. And infinite love and thanks to Mom, Dad, family and friends, and all the Bettie Babes. Much love to all!

Ron: Many thanks to my friends and family—especially my mom, Goldie—for saving all of these treasures over the years. And a very special thank you to Tori Rodriguez for help above and beyond in making this book possible.

Tori and Ron would like to thank Mark Roesler and Bill Uglow of CMG Worldwide for their gracious support of this project, and all the wonderful Bettie fans worldwide!